**Scribe Publications**
## THE NEW FRONT PAGE

Tim Dunlop was a pioneer of political blogging in Australia. He ran the internationally successful independent blog *The Road to Surfdom* and was the first Australian blogger to be hired by a mainstream media organisation (News Limited, for which he wrote the political blog *Blogocracy*). He has a PhD in communication and political philosophy, teaches at Melbourne University, and writes regularly for a number of publications, including *The Drum*. He lives in Melbourne with his wife and son, and tweets at @timdunlop.

# THE NEW FRONT PAGE

## NEW MEDIA AND THE RISE OF THE AUDIENCE

## TIM DUNLOP

SCRIBE

*Melbourne • London*

Scribe Publications Pty Ltd
18–20 Edward St, Brunswick, Victoria 3056, Australia
Email: info@scribepub.com.au

First published by Scribe 2013

Typeset in 12/17 pt Adobe Caslon Pro by the publishers
Printed and bound in Australia by Griffin Press

The paper this book is printed on is certified against the Forest
Stewardship Council® Standards. Griffin Press holds FSC chain
of custody certification SGS-COC-005088. FSC promotes
environmentally responsible, socially beneficial and economically
viable management of the world's forests.

National Library of Australia
Cataloguing-in-Publication data

Dunlop, Tim, author.

The New Front Page: new media and the rise of the audience / Tim Dunlop.

9781922070548 (paperback)
9781922072665 (e-book)

1. Journalism–Social aspects. 2. Online journalism. 3. Digital media.
4. Social change–21st century.

070.4

This project has been assisted by
the Australian Government through
the Australia Council, its arts
funding and advisory body.

scribepublications.com.au

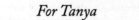

*For Tanya*

# Contents

# INTRODUCTION

## *The Only Show in Town*

*As one Southern publisher famously confessed,*
*'I owe my exalted position in life to two great American*
*institutions — nepotism and monopoly.'*
WARREN BUFFETT, BERKSHIRE HATHAWAY CEO,
IN A LETTER TO INVESTORS

The first story I ever had published in a newspaper was about ASIO. It was 1984 and I was living in Canberra, and I went for a job interview with our domestic intelligence organisation, more out of curiosity than any particular desire to be a spook. I got through the initial, weed-out-the-morons rounds of the process and was invited to ASIO headquarters for a one-on-one interview. I was told to be at the building at two o'clock one particular afternoon, and to go to the canteen.

On the designated day, I went into the foyer and looked around for signs to guide me. There were none. *A-ha*, I remember thinking. This is a test. There must be a clue somewhere. Long minutes passed, but nothing presented itself. As my mind raced, my palms sweated, and my eyes darted, I spotted a woman at the other end of the area I was in, holding a clipboard. Convinced I had already failed my initiation, I walked up to her.

'Excuse me,' I said. 'Can you tell me where the canteen is?'

'I'm the canteen,' she said, and I tried not to laugh.

Maybe it was just that I could never imagine myself using a codename and keeping a straight face, but by the time the interview started, I had already decided that I would never work there. What's more, despite being instructed not to speak to anyone about the day's events, I simply couldn't resist telling the story.

That night, I wrote about the interview on my brand-spanking-new Amiga 500 desktop computer. I printed the story out the next day on a dot-matrix printer (on computer paper, no less, the stuff with perforated edges that you tore off), and, proving just how bad a secret squirrel I would've been, I mailed it off to *The Canberra Times*.

For the next week, I was at the local newsagent every day, desperate to see if the paper would publish it, until suddenly, there it was, on the smudgeable broadsheet pages I held up before me as I stood in the shop. To my amazement, my story was on the front page of their midweek magazine section. It was topped with a big picture by their chief illustrator, and not one word of what I had written had been changed. I bought ten copies and forced them on friends and family. I was at the newsagent the next two days as well, checking to see if the story got any response from readers, and in Friday's paper there were two letters to the editor about it, from how many submitted I didn't know. A few weeks after that, a cheque arrived in the mail, which I took to the bank and cashed.

It all seems so primitive now. A computer so slow you could make a sandwich in the time it took to open its word-processing application. A printer that whirred like a diamond saw cutting concrete. No email and no attachments, and no electronic funds transfer for the payment. And, of course, the only way to read the story at all was to buy a newspaper — with money — and hold it in your hands. No internet, so no *Canberra Times* website and certainly no Twitter or Facebook or Google+ with which to share it with my friends and family, at home, overseas, and interstate, and no way for readers to talk to me, or to talk publicly with each other, about it.

Looking back, the most amazing thing about that period was the institution of the newspaper itself. It seemed ageless and indestructible. Owners would come and go — as they did at *The Canberra Times* — but few people thought that newspapers themselves would ever be anything other than a desirable business proposition, a silver spoon to be passed from one generation of media moguls to the next. And yet, in a very short space of time, it all changed, and not just for newspapers. The advertising that sustained them found other outlets online, and profitability crashed. The content that people had to walk to the shops for and buy is now available — for free in many cases — on their computers, phones, and tablets. Most importantly of all, the audience for journalism is no longer made up of passive consumers; people now actively participate in choosing the stories they want to read and in creating their own content. Social media has become the new front page of journalism, particularly of political journalism, and we are nowhere near the end of this vast experiment in crowdsourcing and public participation.

There is a great quote by British journalist Brian Cathcart in the e-book he wrote in response to the *News of the World* scandal: 'To do [their] job well journalists need to be troublemakers, they need to be noisy and awkward, they need, sometimes, to have the latitude to go too far so that when it counts they have the nerve to go far enough.' I love that. It is basically saying that we need to give journalists enough leeway to be obnoxious and pushy in trivial matters so that they will bring the same level of pushiness to stories that *do* matter. It captures perfectly the paradox we the people face when we try to get our heads around the fact that the media is at once an utter sewer — of lies, exaggeration, sensationalism, slurs, bias, innuendo, and plain incompetence — and a cornerstone of a properly functioning democracy, the institution we ultimately rely upon to hold the powerful in our society to account.

The quote and the paradox it highlights are particularly relevant to the focus of this book. What I intend to discuss in these pages is the relationship between the mainstream media and its audience. I want to try to understand why that relationship is the way it is, and how it is changing because of the intrusion of social media. I want to look at how the internet has destroyed the business model that supported important journalism and has thus forced the media into asking us to pay directly for what it is offering. I also want to discuss how, because of all these changes, the audience's civic and commercial relationship with the media has changed, the audience moving from a passive consumer to a much more active force — a force that can no longer be taken for granted.

My obsession with the relationship between the media and its audience is undoubtedly a by-product of my own working experience. I was raised in retail and had the primacy of the customer drilled into me from an early age. My first jobs, on weekends and during school holidays, were at my father's service station in Canberra, and in those days, they really were *service* stations. When the cars came in, we ran out and cleaned the windscreens, put in the petrol, offered to check the oil and the battery, and pumped up the tyres. We took the money inside to the till and brought the change back to the waiting driver.

Later, when I worked for the big record shop in the centre of town, customer service was again what the bosses demanded. You were polite and you helped people with whatever enquiry they had, no matter how crazy. So when a customer came in looking for a song but they didn't know the artist's name, or the name of the song, or anything else about it except that maybe it had something to do with love, you didn't scoff or laugh — you spent however long it took to figure out what the hell they were talking about. And then you sold it to them.

A couple of years out of school, back in the early 1980s, I opened my first business, one of the first video libraries in Melbourne. My partners and I did our best to figure out what our customers wanted, trying practices that were designed to be customer-friendly, such as longer opening hours and rethinking the industry-standard business model of a one-off, annual fee. We were one of the first stores to offer overnight fees, and we were rewarded with an influx of new customers and a growing bottom line. In fact, by the time Christmas came around in our first year of trading, our customers were bringing us gifts! That sort of thing leaves an indelible mark, and it's a pretty simple lesson you learn: looking after your customers helps you to make money.

But in saying this, I don't want to imply that the relationship between the media and its audience is only about customer service, as important as that is. Editors, publishers, and journalists also have to relate to their audience as citizens. They have to be willing to provide information, analysis, and opinion that meets civic criteria, not market criteria, and that contributes to the democratic life of the nation, not just to the bottom line of a corporation. Of course, this is exactly what those in the media argue they are doing when they claim to be a 'fourth estate', an institution working as a watchdog over the power of other institutions, and much of what I argue in this book is predicated on taking them at their word about that.

So let's go back to that quote about journalists needing to be troublemakers, to be noisy and awkward. How exactly does that understanding of what journalists do sit with the idea of them as service providers to a newly empowered audience?

Traditionally, journalists have been able to indulge an image of themselves as gruff outsiders, indifferent to people's feelings and their criticisms, because the pursuit of truth demanded they be that sort of person — the sort who isn't deterred just because someone says something nasty about them, or demands access to their sources, or threatens them with jail if they won't provide that information. Arguably, such a self-image was and is necessary in order to get the job done, and so being indifferent to the audience is almost part of the job description. It mightn't fit my idea of a good retail relationship with customers, but it never had to — until recently, journalism was supported by a business model that didn't require journalists to have that sort of relationship with those who consumed its products.

In the past, journalists were able to think of themselves as messengers — mere bearers of information. But it is precisely this self-image that the new-media environment has challenged. More and more, journalists no longer have proprietorial control of 'the news', thanks to the availability online of the raw material they use to build their stories — the footage of a media conference on YouTube or live on ABC News 24, the press release on the minister's website, the images of confrontation in Tahrir Square being linked live via Twitter. An audience that has access to this sort of information in real time is not going to be able to ignore the role the media plays in shaping the news it reports; nor is it going to be possible for the media to ignore the active role the audience can play in shaping its own experience of the news.

Asked once why her songs were always about herself, Joni Mitchell denied that to be the case. Real life doesn't rhyme, she insisted. No it doesn't, but journalists, like songwriters, are in the rhyming business. They purport to make sense of the world for us, and in so doing they tend to knock off the rough edges and leave out the bits that don't fit the metre of the story they are telling. They don't just report; they create. I don't mean this in some weird postmodern way where truth is either relative or non-existent. Nor do I mean that journalists set out to deceive or even actively lie (though as the Leveson Inquiry in Britain has shown us, in pursuit of a story they will often jettison ethical concerns). I mean it in the more everyday sense — they *mediate* information for us. They choose which stories to tell us about. They choose which stories get prominence and which are relegated to the inside pages, or spiked altogether. They construct stories, narratives, that profess to connect and make sense of events. They decide whose views to share with us, and whose to ignore. When it comes to the great avalanche of information crashing down upon them every day, they are selective, necessarily so.

In the pre-internet age, the audience more or less had to accept their choices. Today they don't.

But this isn't the only thing that has changed between the media and its audience. In the traditional media business model, readers of newspapers, watchers of television, and listeners to radio were never seen as customers in the way most businesses understand that term. The media didn't consider its audience as customers so much as a product. The audience was the thing they sold to advertisers. In the same way that factories produced widgets, media organisations produced punters (as they are often called within the industry) — the people who lined up to watch or listen to the shows and to read the newspapers. It was a pretty effective arrangement, and it made many in the industry rich and powerful, and conferred upon them influence and prestige. But it was also the media's original sin. It created a fraught relationship between the audience and the media, and how could it not? After all, if your audience is really just the product you are generating in order to on-sell to advertisers, you are likely to think of them as something you can manipulate so as to maximise your profit. You are going to think of them in aggregate, as demographic categories, not as a collection of individuals whose needs you have to satisfy and to whose demands you have to respond.

Looking back on it now, it seems incredible that a major industry could so completely fool itself about the nature of its relationship with its audience. The media's self-deception was sustained by two pillars, and these pillars helped to hide what was happening to the industry for much longer than should have been the case.

The first pillar was that mainstream media outlets had little competition. It was so expensive to start a newspaper, or a television or radio station, that few were able to enter the market. As veteran American journalist Philip Meyer noted in a 2013 interview about newspapers:

> [They] peaked around 1920, when 130 papers were sold for every 100 households. Then other media, starting with radio, began taking business away. That process accelerated when Google and Craig Newmark discovered in the 1990s that the Internet was a highly efficient advertising medium. Newspapers coped through most of the 20th century by consolidating down to one paper in most markets and using monopoly power to control prices.

Australia might just be the ultimate example of this sort of consolidation, where the market is controlled by a few big players, to the extent that ours is considered the most concentrated media market in the free world.

This ability to dominate the market gave these businesses an enormous advantage, and they used it ruthlessly to protect their position. They pressured governments to favour them with protective legislation, and they used their market share to milk top dollar from advertisers and to keep would-be competitors at bay. But crucially, it also meant that they could ignore their audience because theirs was the only show in town. The relationship was primed for exploitation, pure and simple.

No business likes to think of itself as exploitative, so mass media outlets needed to be able to rationalise the way they treated their audience. Media organisations thus collectively presented themselves as a democratic watchdog providing a service that the public valued and needed, rather than as an industry corralling an audience it then flogged off to soap and toothpaste manufacturers. This was the second pillar, and the media still revels in the idea that it is the fourth estate, the guardian of democracy that relentlessly pursues truth in the face of the obfuscations of governments and the rich and powerful. And there is just enough evidence that it *is* this noble thing for the claim to be convincing. Watergate or the Pentagon Papers, the Moonlight State exposé, or even the exposure of the *News of the World* scandal are prime examples of this sort of watchdog role, and there are many more everyday instances of good investigative journalism — look no further than *The Age* Investigative Unit, for example — to convince the media of its basic integrity and that it is playing an important civic role in the life of democratic nations.

The fact that the media became exactly the sort of rich and powerful institution that it believed itself to be keeping watch over did very little to undermine its belief in its own exceptionalism, and that belief allowed it to rationalise away all its other shortcomings. Yes, media outlets said, we might produce an inordinate amount of celebrity gossip and sport, we might be obsessed with the theatre of politics at the expense of the substance, we might ignore stories that cast our proprietors in a dubious light, but, remember Watergate!

Some within the industry go so far as to argue that the low end of journalism — the scandal, the celebrity gossip, the tattle-tale stories of sleaze and salaciousness — is a necessary precondition for the high-end journalism that they so often cite as their 'real' role. Paul Dacre, editor of the *Daily Mail* in Britain, one of the highest circulation newspapers in the world, told the UK Society of Editors in 2008 that 'if mass-circulation newspapers, which also devote considerable space to reporting and analysis of public affairs, don't have the freedom to write about scandal, I doubt whether they will retain their mass circulations, with the obvious worrying implications for the democratic process'.

This is either a hard-headed account of the industry by a business realist, or the perfect illustration of the low opinion in which the media holds not only its audience but also its own ability to perform its civic function in a way that attracts an audience. Perhaps it is both, in which case it is more realistic to reverse Dacre's notion of cause and effect: rather than the scandal and sleaze being necessary to pay for the investigative journalism, the investigative journalism is the fig leaf used to cover the media's obsession with sleaze and scandal. In other words, the fourth-estate archetype has helped to reinforce the media's original-sin relationship with its audience, and the audience has never had much of a chance to respond.

But all this began to change with the invention of the internet. As readers migrated online, circulation of the physical newspaper dwindled. Online display advertising was worth a lot less than its paper equivalent because advertisers could now count how many people paid attention to their ads. Classified advertising found a new home on various websites, some of which, like craigslist, actually ran for free. The media's business model collapsed.

Just as importantly, we reached the Skynet moment: the audience became self-aware and demanded a say in how the factory was run. Blogs sprang up like photographers at a celebrity wedding, social media thrived, and comments boxes on news stories filled up. The passive recipients of what the media had been offering suddenly became active participants in the production and dissemination of news. The internet not only dissolved print media's control of classified advertising and the 'rivers of gold' that they had happily and carelessly splashed around in since Gutenberg was a boy, but it also provided the audience with a way of talking back to the people who had for so long treated them as widgets and democratic supplicants.

A world of pain followed. The media wasn't the only industry to have its verities called into question by the rise and rise of the internet, but it was subjected to a particular species of trouble that no other industry has had to endure: as well as its business model being rendered inadequate, the media's self-image as a provider of wisdom, insight, and truth — in short, its authority — was stripped. Its presumptions about its relationship with its audience evaporated like spit on a griddle.

Iraq proved to be a turning point. Not only did much of the mainstream media fail to see behind the false case presented by the Bush administration for the invasion, but they were also *shown* to have failed in that basic duty by the so-called new media, the endless stream of blogs that blossomed in the lead-up to and prosecution of that war. If the mainstream media could get the reporting wrong on something as important as a war, when mere amateurs could see through the nonsense, what else was it getting wrong? That was the question a key segment of the audience suddenly asked themselves, and they've been asking it daily ever since. What's more, social media has provided them with the means to ask the question publicly. Consequently, the media has been exposed to the sort of scrutiny it usually directs at others.

The failures in reporting on Iraq led not just to a collapse in trust between the media and its audience, but also to open hostility between new media and old; some might even say to paranoia from the old guard. The net effect of this was that the mainstream media, instead of attending to its own problems and attempting to fix them, projected its failures onto new-media practitioners and thus delayed by at least a decade the necessary rethink of its business that the new environment demanded. The mainstream found itself attacking that part of the citizenry and its audience most engaged with the journalism it was providing — a truly incredible situation for the industry to find itself in at the exact moment it was asking those same people to pay directly for its product.

The *News of the World* scandal was the other shoe dropping. It showed an industry so intent on rounding up an audience to sell to advertisers that journalists and editors were not only willing to harass celebrities, threaten politicians, and illegally pay police for information, but they were also actually willing to hack into the voicemail of a kidnapped — and subsequently murdered — schoolgirl and write stories based on what they found in that inner sanctum. This was not a sign of healthy competition, and it certainly was not the fearless investigative reporting that had sustained the myth of the fourth estate. It was the pathological behaviour of a major section of the industry inured to indecency. What happened at *News of the World* could only have occurred in an organisation that had lost any sense of social responsibility or genuine understanding of how to treat its audience. They kidded themselves, as the media often does, that they were giving the people what they wanted, but when the people found out what was happening, they petitioned the paper's advertisers, and *News of the World* had no choice but to close in disgrace.

Of course, not every news organisation is guilty of the excesses of *News of the World*. Indeed, we should remember that it was another media group, *The Guardian*, that exposed the corruption at *News of the World*, in precisely the way that the fourth estate is meant to. This means that no easy lessons can be learned, and no simple moral can be extracted. Certainly, the new media, the 'citizen journalists' of self-constructed legend, cannot just step in and replace the (allegedly) dying old media. Nonetheless, it is reasonable to conclude that although what happened at *News of the World* was extreme, it was different only in intensity, not kind, from the sort of thing that news organisations do every day in the name of wrangling an audience for their advertisers.

The question to ask now is whether lessons have been learned. Will the media, the newspaper industry in particular, stop treating their audience solely as a commodity; will they use the new technology to help rebuild trust and credibility? Will they engage with people in a way that not only builds a sustainable business model, but that recasts the media–audience relationship as one between equals?

Some media organisations are starting to at least acknowledge the new environment. We can be encouraged, for example, by this note from Brett Clegg, the publisher and editor-in-chief of *The Australian Financial Review* (a Fairfax newspaper):

> There are plenty of news sources competing for your time. We have to earn your loyalty. We have to deliver around the clock and we have to meet your information needs.

We don't just report on business and the market – we are a business too and we are responsive to our market – you. There is no standing still for any of us.

And we know we have had to step up our performance.

But on the other hand, we have another Fairfax executive, the CEO and publisher of Fairfax Digital, Jane Huxley, telling industry mag *mUmBRELLA* that they are planning on making their new business model dependent on annoying their audience. No, I'm not joking. As anyone who uses a Fairfax site knows, they allow autoplay advertisements, videos, and pop-ups that start the moment you click through to the site. But rather than respond rationally to the fact that this feature annoys their customers, Fairfax have decided to exploit it: readers can turn the autoplay off, but only by logging in. In this way, the company can collect demographic data to help market itself and yes, on-sell for profit. 'If you log in, your user experience will be enhanced,' Huxley told *mUmBRELLA*. '[I]f you do not log in, your reception will be less warm.'

Huxley's comments suggest that the idea of the customer-as-product, with no acknowledgement that they are also a valued consumer, is still deeply ingrained in the media's psyche. It is hard to imagine another business that would value its customers' goodwill so lightly (okay, banks).

But I remain hopeful, if for no other reason than that the technology isn't going away, and an empowered audience is not going to stop using it.

The focus of this book is the struggle for relevance between the media and its audience, a contest that has both a commercial and a civic aspect. But my bigger point is that this is really just a proxy for a more fundamental struggle between ordinary people — the general public, for want of a better term — and all the other sources of power in a modern democracy that seek to define and influence the sort of society in which we live. The audience can no longer be taken for granted, and the future success of the sort of journalism that contributes to the civic life of the nation depends on the media forging a new compact with its audience. This, in turn, will have ramifications for the general public and their ability to influence power more broadly.

What I present in this book comes very much from the point of view of a member of the audience, but I also document how I came to straddle two roles, both as a customer of the mainstream media and as a contributor to it. Although I don't want to extrapolate too much from my own experience, the simple truth is that more and more people are on both sides of the fence. Social media has allowed each of us to be an audience member and a content provider, and that is simply the terrain the mainstream media has to deal with.

The early chapters of the book document how I became involved with blogging and how this led to a job with News Limited. Chapter one focuses on the pivotal role that Fairfax journalist Margo Kingston played in developing the form via her site *Webdiary*. It was arguably Australia's first political blog, and it gave many readers, including me, their first opportunity to be published in this new electronic form. It was certainly the first mainstream site in Australia to open up a legitimate dialogue between journalist and audience. Chapter two explains how bloggers like me got our start, how we coped with the technology, and how we helped to invent a particular relationship with our audiences. Chapter three explores how the blogosphere became professionalised, and how that was in some ways both the fulfilment of a dream and the death of an ideal. Chapter four provides some detail on the difficulties involved in running a highly trafficked comments section, and what online discussion means for public debate more generally. Chapters five and six deal with some of the specific ways in which the media attempts to define the audience, and I look at the claims made about so-called trolling and echo chambers, suggesting that many of them are in fact examples of the media trying to reassert the status quo, against the interests of its audience. Chapter seven looks at the audience itself, and attempts to understand what the demographic data shows us about its composition. In particular, I take a close look at the assertion that ordinary citizens are disengaged from politics, another claim the media uses to justify the gossipy stories it often produces.

The book is highly critical of the way in which many in the media deal with and relate to their audiences, but it is criticism that comes from a genuine desire to see the industry thrive, not disappear. And as fed up as I am with the way many journalists and editors treat their audiences, I am also happy to acknowledge that there is a new wave of tech-savvy editors and journalists — some of whom I've been lucky enough to work with — who understand the changes and who understand the primacy of the audience. The difficulty they face is that they are part of an industry in which old habits die hard. The impediments to reinvention are massive because they are structural and cultural: they are barnacled onto the DNA of the industry, while the industry itself is embedded in a particular set of societal relationships that are also resistant to change.

The internet and all it has wrought is not going away, and in such an environment, where journalism will utterly depend on its ability to attract paying customers in order to support itself, the relationship between the media and its audience becomes vital.

But it goes even deeper than that. We live in a time where many of our key institutions, from churches to the government to the media itself, have lost the trust and respect of ordinary people. This has happened because the elites that run such organisations are increasingly isolated from the views of those they allegedly serve. My intention is not to pick apart the reasons for this isolation, only to suggest that the situation is not going to improve until we have a media that can properly deal with the rise of the audience and better provide citizens with the information they need in order to participate meaningfully in public debate. As British author Dan Hind says in his book *The Return of the Public*, it is only '[b]y changing the institutional structures through which we generate and share information we begin to set ourselves free, since only a world more fully and more widely understood can be transformed'.

Let's talk about that transformation.

## CHAPTER ONE

# The Mainstream Goes Online

*We pretend that our present system is democratic,
yet the people never have the chance nor the means to express
their views on any problem of public life. Any issue that does
not pertain to particular interests is abandoned to collective
passions, which are systematically and officially inflamed.*

SIMONE WEIL, PHILOSOPHER AND SOCIAL ACTIVIST

I was in Year 10 at school in Canberra when the governor-general, Sir John Kerr, sacked the Whitlam government and installed Malcolm Fraser as caretaker prime minister in 1975. Our class was in the library at the time. Some of the kids were into politics — this was Canberra, after all — and they looked positively shocked as history leaked out of Parliament House a few suburbs away and reached us where we stood among the bookshelves. But I remember being pretty indifferent. My family, unlike most in the nation's capital, didn't work in government, didn't have anything to do with it outside their citizenship. They were small-business owners and lifelong conservatives, and I think to the extent that I gave the matter any serious thought, 15-year-old me probably considered it pretty funny that Gough Whitlam had been kicked out of office. But you couldn't live in Canberra at that time and not be touched by the moment as it rushed by. The long days of debate and introspection, argument, heartbreak, joy, and partisanship that followed echo through our politics to this day. It was a defining moment, even if some of us were too obsessed with Emerson, Lake and Palmer, and Led Zeppelin to notice that we were being defined.

Twenty years later, when a fish-and-chip shop owner from Queensland was elected to federal parliament, and all hell broke loose in the political establishment and in the recently roused electorates, there was much talk about what a threat Pauline Hanson was to our democracy, how she diminished us and exposed our country's allegedly racist underbelly, how she made us a laughing-stock in the eyes of the world, and how something just had to be done about her. By then I was paying much closer attention to such matters, and although I abhorred just about everything Hanson stood for, I couldn't get the foam of outrage to form at the corners of my mouth. Yes, God help us, she was saying awful things, but the idea that an ordinary woman from the suburbs putting herself forward for election, winning a seat, and then running around the country speaking in public about her views was a threat to our democracy was a proposition of self-evident stupidity.

In both the Dismissal and the rise and fall of Pauline Hanson, Australian society played out an age-old argument about the relationship between the governed and the governors, the elite and the ordinary people, the empowered and the powerless. The same arguments would arise during later debates about the economic reforms of the Hawke and Keating years, the discussions surrounding the Iraq War and WorkChoices, and those around a price on carbon and a tax on mining. They clatter through every debate in a democracy because that is what democracy is, ultimately: an argument about how the spoils of society are shared, who controls them, and who gets to have a say about how these things are sorted out. For the most part, the division of labour between the governed and the governors seems settled, almost natural, and everyone goes about their business as if it is; it is only when big events and phenomena such as Hanson or the Dismissal occur that we realise what seemed like a natural settlement was nothing more than a pause in an ongoing battle.

Ours is a representative democracy, where we elect people to worry about the minutiae of actually running the country. Most people's day-to-day involvement in the machinations of government is outsourced to the political class — not only the politicians themselves but also the bureaucrats, advisers, policy experts, party hacks, and all the rest of them — in a vast apparatus that constitutes the private and public face of the state. The other key members of this class are journalists — particularly the political journalists, who literally mediate the running of the country through their newspaper articles, their opinion columns, their television programs, and their radio shows.

In his book *The Media We Deserve,* journalist David Salter puts it this way: '[I]t might be more sensible to argue that the media have become so pervasive and powerful that they may be beginning to supplant reality itself ... They decide — on the basis of habit, prejudice and commercial interest — what we should know and what we need not.' The filters they employ in doing so become invisible, and so journalists come to believe that they are merely messengers. They also come to believe that they are objective, and their profession has developed a number of practices designed to ensure that objectivity.

Most of us join in the illusion: we accept what we read in the paper or see on the nightly news as the truth. Pushed, I'm sure most people would recognise that there is a certain amount of manipulation going on, and certainly years of opinion polls suggest that we don't think the media can be trusted. But such are the structural constraints on our ability to take such intuitions to their logical conclusion that we simply go with the flow. Absent some compelling reason to look more closely — such as a Dismissal or a Hanson — we allow a convenient simplification like this, that the media is telling the truth, to enable us to carry on our complicated lives.

We happily outsource our ability to watch those who govern us to journalists because we need them to do it for us. We understand in our democratic marrow that not only is a free press a necessary part of a free society, but also that we, as individuals, just do not have the time or resources to do what we ask the media to do; we cannot monitor power in the way that an institutionalised free press can. (The whole contemporary fantasy of the 'citizen journalist' is based upon ignoring this reality.) So we accept their version of events as the truth, and there is nothing untoward about any of this. We are not failing as citizens by entering into such an understanding — but we should not kid ourselves that this arrangement is without its problems.

The media are often accused of political bias, and that is certainly an issue, but their real power lies in the fact that they get to choose what we care about. Even today, with Twitter and Facebook and blogs and all other forms of social media going full steam 24 hours a day, with all their pontificating and joking, linking and liking, analysis and demolition and whinging, it is still the choices made by the mainstream media about what is important that dominates such discussions. It doesn't matter how many polls there are that show that we don't like or trust the media, it doesn't matter how often kids at school or students at university learn about the way that the media manipulates information, and it doesn't matter how savvy a generation of 'digital natives' becomes; at the end of the day, there is just something compelling and powerful about the 'news', as chosen by the mainstream media. A headline on the front page of *The Daily Telegraph* that says 'Boat Backflip: asylum open-door policy' is a much more serious (some might say insidious) and influential thing than a carefully argued blog post that shows how misleading the article is.

As it happens, the Hanson moment in Australian politics was very close in time to the beginning of a great technological disruption: the digitisation of news via the technologies associated with the internet. The two events coincided in a way that has some relevance for the discussion in this book. The new technologies provided journalists with tools that for the first time allowed them to step outside the usual relationship they had with their audience, and one journalist in particular seized the moment with gusto. It may not have seemed so at the time, but in hindsight it is clear that it was a seminal moment for the Australian media, and it showed many of us what might be possible.

In 1996, a leading journalist working at Fairfax as part of the press gallery had something of an epiphany when Pauline Hanson came on the scene. The journalist was Margo Kingston, and the revelation was that she and her colleagues had not been describing reality properly. In the introduction to her book *Off the Rails*, an account of Hanson's failed re-election campaign in 1998, Kingston writes:

> [A]ny honest look at the disillusion in the Australian political landscape has to face up to the media's complicity — inadvertent and otherwise — in the gamesmanship of the electoral process. The leaders and journalists are actors in a play, bound by intricate codes of etiquette and self-interest.

We pick their spin, they pick ours, and both sides look only at each other, as journalists present our theatre reviews to an ever more disconnected public. Little wonder that the public has come to distrust us, the media, as much as the politicians.

Kingston, tired and disillusioned after the experience of covering Hanson's campaign, was planning to get herself transferred to the country town of Bourke in New South Wales so that she could report on rural and Aboriginal matters. 'I wanted to be an insider on the outside,' she told me in an interview in November 2012, 'and compare the policies coming out of Canberra with what was happening on the ground.'

The plan was nixed by her editor Paul McGeough, who asked her to return to her former role as chief of staff for Fairfax's Canberra bureau. 'That was a very big favour to ask,' Kingston said, 'because it's a shithouse job, all responsibility and little real power.'

She agreed to do it, but in return asked to be able to write her own column, something she had been denied up until that point in her career, despite being in demand for appearances on various radio and television programs. McGeough agreed, and so Kingston began another stint as chief of staff in Canberra.

In early 2000, before her column could be organised, something unexpected happened: Fairfax's head of online media, Tom Burton, offered the Canberra-based Kingston an online column. 'He was head of smh.com.au and he was very cutting edge and always wanting to experiment,' Kingston recalled. Burton rang and asked Kingston if she wanted to have an online column, to which she responded, 'What's that?' She told him that she knew nothing about computers 'and all that' and she really had no idea what he was offering. 'He told me, Look, it's all done for you. We'll call it *Webdiary* if that's all right with you, and you just do it when you feel like it. Just write something and then press this button and it's published.'

The whole concept bewildered Kingston, from the lack of a deadline to the push-button publication process, but she was keen to have a space somewhere within Fairfax where she could express an opinion, so Burton's proposal, as alien as it seemed on one level, was attractive. 'Tom said, We'll put your email address at the bottom and people can email you with their response, and I said, No, I don't want that. I had to have a silent number after Hanson as there were a few very weird people and so I didn't want to have any reader involvement. Tom said, I want to just try it out and see what happens. And once it started and I got my first emails, I thought, I've got a chance to do something here.'

American journalist Dan Froomkin wrote the following in a 2009 piece for the *Nieman Journalism Lab*. He tweeted a link to it in 2012, saying that this was still a lesson the industry needed to learn:

> If we were to start an online newspaper from scratch today, we'd recognize that toneless, small-bore news stories are not

the way to build a large audience — not even with 'interactive' bells and whistles cobbled on top. One option might be to imitate cable TV, and engage in a furious volume of he-said/she-said reporting, voyeurism, contrarianism, gossip, triviality and gotcha journalism. But that would come at the cost of our souls. The right way to reinvent ourselves online would be to do precisely what journalists were put on this green earth to do: Seek the truth, hold the powerful accountable, expose the B.S., explain how things really work, introduce people to each other, and tell compelling stories. And we should do all those things passionately and courageously — not hiding who we are, but rather engaging in a very public expression of our journalistic values.

It is a startling quote because what Froomkin describes is what *Webdiary* put into practice a decade ahead of his explanation. What he describes, and what *Webdiary* delivered, is the sort of journalism that fundamentally alters the relationship between the media and its audience; the sort of journalism that breaks the fourth wall between journalists and citizens, the force field that keeps the two separate. This is an approach that, depending on your point of view, is either going to save journalism or destroy it.

*Webdiary* went live in July 2000 and I stumbled across it accidentally. I was in the midst of writing a doctoral thesis in which I was trying to say something useful about the role of intellectuals and citizens in public debate. The discussion wasn't limited to Australia, and I was drawing on all sorts of political philosophy and sociological understandings of what exactly an intellectual was, but I was struck by the way in which the Australian literature made light of the possibility that we could even have intellectuals. The tone was set by Donald Horne in *The Lucky Country*:

> Australia has never had a cultivated leisure class and lacks one now. There are no periodicals or quality press, so that people get away with expressing things that would not be tolerated in more sophisticated societies; politicians go unsatirised. Intellectuals, in the sense of creative thinkers who are publicly influential, simply do not exist in Australia.

In fairness, Horne's view was probably more nuanced than that single quote implies, but it was the unnuanced version that persisted in the literature. 'Australian intellectual' was often presented as an oxymoron.

What I hated about that was not just that it was demonstrably wrong, but also that it reeked of the sort of colonial, cringing attitude that extended to public debate as a whole. If our betters thought that our intellectuals were dumb, second-rate hacks, imagine what they thought of the rest of us. My thesis was aimed at coming up with an understanding that not only challenged this outdated view of intellectual life in Australia, but that also rethought the whole relationship between intellectuals — those with either expertise or some other privileged access to public discussion — and the rest of the population.

But even as it stood staring me in the face, I completely missed the significance of *Webdiary*. In fact, I was quite suspicious of the whole notion, from the moment I read the first piece Kingston posted:

Welcome to my Canberra diary. I'm allowed to say what I think whenever I like, and lucky you can interact if you like. The downside for this indulgence is that all the words stay forever so I can be judged for my sins.

If this weird idea survives, I'm going to lobby for the … techheads to add a program called 'MPoll', where I'll ask a question and you can vote (and suggest your own). I'll send the results to whoever is responsible for the question or the answer and publish their response, if any.

What did she mean we could 'interact' with her? What did she mean she could write what she liked? If she was allowed to say what she thought in *Webdiary*, what was she saying in articles published elsewhere?

Looking back on it now, I realise I didn't trust her. Here was a journalist telling me that she was starting the sort of project that thesis-me, citizen-me would consider a good and desirable thing, but I simply didn't believe her. I can distinctly remember being quite cross about the whole thing, as if she were trying to put one over on me. It is perhaps a measure of the disadvantage that all new journalistic endeavours begin with, given the low standing the profession has with the public at large, that they first have to overcome this trust deficit just to get people to pay attention, let alone give them the benefit of the doubt. And I know this seems to contradict what I wrote earlier about people presuming that what they read in the newspaper or see on the nightly news is the truth, but that is the paradox. The media is so embedded in a particular understanding most of us have of our society that we *do* tend to presume that they are, within certain parameters, telling the truth. How could they be allowed to lie to us? we wonder. On a day-to-day basis we don't give the matter much conscious thought; but when something comes along that forces us to really think about what they are doing, our scepticism is engaged.

Talking to Kingston and others associated with *Webdiary*, it became apparent that the site was a seat-of-the-pants operation, especially in its early days. It is also hard to overstate just how marginal online journalism was in the scheme of things at Fairfax (or at any other news organisation). 'I didn't have a clue about it,' Kingston said. 'All I knew was that Tom [Burton] ran this funny thing. I mean, I never looked at the *Herald* online site. No journo did. It was on its own, with these wild people doing these wild music things, and a rugby column or something.'

Kingston's online editor at the time, Stephen Hutcheon, concurred. 'Online wasn't taken seriously. We started out as a bunch of ne'er-do-wells, lost souls, burnt-out subs, and copy kids eager to break into journalism.'

In fact, truth be told, *Webdiary* was in large part Fairfax's solution to a perceived problem — Margo Kingston. Management saw her as a maverick, and there was a desire to rein her in. As Hutcheon explained: 'Ever since I've known Margo … she has pushed that line of demarcation to the extreme. While it didn't worry me as much, it pissed off a lot of the senior editorial management at the time. And to be fair, they were the ones that fielded the complaints.'

Kingston understood how she was viewed: 'There were clearly complaints about my coverage coming from politicians because I was playing hard.'

But despite Fairfax management's view of *Webdiary*, Kingston embraced her new ghetto. From the beginning, she was almost painfully transparent about what she was doing. She knew that 'by some strange and mysterious quirk of fate' she had been given 'this rare and extraordinary opportunity to write and edit my own work and to be totally responsible for every aspect of it and to have complete freedom to write what I liked'. But she also knew that this meant she had to have 'a very strict policy' on ethics. 'I wanted readers to know that if I got something wrong I would correct immediately and that any conflict of interest I would disclose and that I would hold myself accountable if someone picked up something that I hadn't done.'

Over time, *Webdiary* began to win me over. It did so because of Kingston's openness. She engaged. She published comments — even lengthy articles — from her readers, and she argued with them in good faith. She did her best to address their concerns. The key was that she grasped the difference between online and conventional newspaper journalism: the relationship with her audience. There were plenty of times when I thought she was wrong about things, but big deal. We were there for the discussion, not to have our prejudices pandered to, and so she pushed back against what we said and allowed us to argue with each other. The interactions weren't always satisfactory; I was never happy, for instance, about her willingness to allow anonymous attacks on those of us who wrote under our real names, and I told her as much many times as I began to use the site more frequently. But the experimental nature of what she was doing was well understood by those involved, and so lots of slack was cut. It was close to exactly what Froomkin argued would be the ideal if journalists were starting an online paper from scratch today: 'not hiding who we are, but rather engaging in a very public expression of our journalistic values'.

When I interviewed Kingston in 2012, I asked her if she had previously thought much about the relationship between journalists and readers. 'I feel that I was woken up about it,' she said. 'I was always what would be considered a romantic journalist, [believing] that we were there on behalf of the people. But I didn't actually live it, and the evidence of that is when Pauline Hanson gave her maiden speech, I thought she should be ignored. But then I forced myself to experience the audience by covering her in depth, and I wrote the book about it. The question I got from the Hanson campaign and all those weird things that happened was, can we actually find a space for civil discourse between opposing views?

'Once I understood that, and once people started writing in to *Webdiary*, I just thought, okay, I've a got a chance to put this theory into practice. I thought journalism had to change.'

But at the same time as she was becoming comfortable with the form, Kingston was also being blindsided by how much people mistrusted journalists, something that became apparent once she started interacting with readers at *Webdiary*. 'I was shocked. And I think it was because I subconsciously exempted myself. I felt that I was definitely okay, that people would trust me. But they didn't.'

This conflict goes to the heart of the media's image of itself as a profession, its understanding of its role in the formation of public opinion, and, most importantly, its understanding of the source of its power, as both a gatekeeper deciding who gets to participate, and as interpreter of the national conversation. Once you let the audience in as an equal player, much of that power dissipates.

That was precisely what brought Kingston's role as chief of staff in Canberra and her role as sole organiser of *Webdiary* into irreconcilable conflict. A large part of what her managers didn't like was that she discussed with her readers her opinions about which questions journalists should have been asking. 'The Peter Reith telecard affair was probably the earliest case, up close and personal, of where I'd get the readers involved in the actual internal workings of the bureau,' Kingston told me. (In the incident Kingston is referring to, Peter Reith, the minister for workplace relations, gave his son the pin number to his parliamentary telephone account, and the son, and some others who gained access to the pin, ran up a bill of some $50,000 at the taxpayers' expense.) 'I went in hard on that. Very, very hard. And some at Fairfax didn't like it ... I'd say on *Webdiary*, "The *Herald* has just sent this list of questions to Peter Reith. This is what he needs to answer."'

I was stunned to hear that a media organisation was concerned about a journalist 'going in hard'. I asked Kingston, isn't that what you're all meant to do? Isn't the job to go in hard? 'Well,' she replied, 'that's the theory, but it's not the way it is.'

Kingston came under pressure to stop running with the story. 'In retrospect, that led to me resigning as chief of staff, because it got so tense. I got so overwhelmed having to do full-time chief of staff and *Webdiary* that I had a bit of a meltdown. I needed to take time out.'

It seems the only reason she kept her job at this stage was that Tom Burton intervened on her behalf, suggesting she could be deployed as part of the online team, where she could contribute and learn the ropes. 'But from the minute I got to Sydney,' Kingston recalled, 'I didn't learn about any of the online operation. I just focused on *Webdiary*, and that's when it became my full-time job.'

Historically, it is important to understand that *Webdiary* was seen as a marginal site within a marginal division being run by an increasingly marginalised journalist. The involvement of readers in generating the content only added to its marginality. The site had few friends within Fairfax, and I was surprised when I asked Kingston about the sort of response she received from her peers, other journalists at Fairfax. 'None,' she said. 'They didn't read it. It wasn't in the psyche. I honestly think it was considered irrelevant. Not where the big game was.'

Still, some momentum had begun to develop. Kingston was working in close proximity to the online editor and other staff, and there was inevitably interaction between them. They began linking to *Webdiary* content, including content written by its readers, via the front page of the *Sydney Morning Herald* website. (For instance, a piece I wrote on dairy deregulation was linked off the front page, and it generated some interest — including an exchange between me and former Labor politician Mark Latham that ended with him declaring that I was an agrarian socialist!)

Kingston pointed out that traffic to the site was relatively small but, 'It became almost a completely transparent space. I'd say, "I think I'd better do something about this, what do you reckon?" I'd write a comment piece, but then the readers would go off and blast me, or come up with a different view, and there'd be a debate.'

It wasn't easy. The technology, by today's standards, was primitive. There were no simple control panels on the backend, as there are today on various blogging programs, allowing people to easily format a piece for online publication. All the coding had to be done by hand, a big ask for someone without the technical training. What's more, all of Kingston's contact with readers happened via email, as there was no comments facility; that technology was not yet invented.

Despite all this, the site was breaking new ground. The *Tampa* incident, in particular, changed Kingston's understanding of what was possible. 'I'll never forget *Tampa*. It was just brilliant. I'd post all this stuff, maybe five huge posts on *Tampa*, and I'd sit there till midnight and be ready to go home and there'd be another pile of emails coming through.

'Who am I to say I have to go home and sleep? Besides, I know if I do that, I come back in the morning there'll be a hundred and fifty waiting for me.'

Kingston saw *Webdiary* as the only place in the mainstream media that was giving voice to dissenting opinion on the topic. 'I felt such a responsibility because it was crystal clear that the people writing in wanted to be on the public record as dissenting. Because they were in such a minority.'

This was a confronting position to take, and it caused concerns at Fairfax. I must say, too, that to me, as a reader, the pages and pages of complaint about *Tampa* that *Webdiary* published did end up looking like a fairly mindless, anti-Australian barrage. I was sympathetic to the contributors' views, but I nonetheless felt strongly enough about the tone and volume of what was being published to email in my concerns about it. I made the point that the 'all Australians are racist' sentiment that pervaded much of the material Kingston was publishing was self-serving and that maybe people could be a bit more focused in their approach. The email was published, but was pretty soon buried and forgotten.

What is interesting is that despite sharing so many principles and practices with independent blogs, Kingston felt that she was still very much a part of the newspaper and the mainstream media. 'I was consciously trying to develop something that would allow integration to the paper,' she told me. 'I never saw myself as part of the blogging world. I saw myself as part of *The Sydney Morning Herald*.'

I suggested to Kingston that, from an outsider's point of view, this differentiation between what she was doing and the blogosphere was odd. Her response was unequivocal. 'Well, there had to be [a distinction],' she said. 'We're a big company. We are read.' But while she was very aware of her site being part of *The Sydney Morning Herald*, she was nonetheless willing to use the relative freedom it provided her within that mainstream structure to pursue journalism in a way that was, it has to be said, groundbreaking.

Yet by 2004, *Webdiary* was accumulating the sort of management concerns that no employee is likely to survive long term, despite the fact that the site was increasingly attracting a decent readership and was providing readers with access unmatched elsewhere in the mainstream media. As well, Kingston was in constant demand for media appearances: not only did she have her regular spot on Phillip Adams' radio show *Late Night Live*, but she was a sought-after guest on programs such as *Lateline*.

Pressure was coming from all sorts of areas. Kingston had published a post in which journalist Antony Loewenstein and Greens member of the New South Wales upper house Ian Cohen each wrote about their response to the fact that Palestinian scholar and activist Dr Hanan Ashrawi had been awarded the Sydney Peace Prize. Both articles wrote in favour of Ashrawi receiving the prize, and the issue provoked an outcry on *Webdiary* (and throughout the media generally). Much to Kingston's surprise, the pieces by Loewenstein and Cohen disappeared from the site. At first she thought it was a technical glitch, but she was eventually told they had been pulled. The reason she was given was that *The Sydney Morning Herald* had received complaints from a number of prominent Jewish readers saying that the pieces were anti-Semitic. According to Kingston, she was told that in such circumstances the first reaction is to remove the offending pieces. She was stunned. After some robust discussion, the pieces were reposted, but the incident was indicative of the resistance she was meeting.

Fairfax management was also receiving complaints about Kingston from within the federal government, including from the office of Prime Minister John Howard. Going into the 2004 federal election campaign, Kingston was touring the country promoting her book *Not Happy, John*, in which she made the case that the Howard government was undermining Australian democracy through deceptions associated with the Iraq War and other examples of what she saw as curtailments of free speech. Although her publishers had, at Kingston's suggestion, set up a website dedicated to the book — the first time an Australian book had been promoted in this way — *Webdiary* nonetheless became ground zero for discussion of the book and its thesis.

Not happy, Margo, was the response from Fairfax management. 'They're dealing with an activist reporter who they have control over, so of course they're getting fucking complaints from Howard,' she told me. 'I mean, wouldn't you [complain] if you were Howard?'

As *Crikey* commented at the time, 'The *Herald* editors just wish Margo would go away ... Kingston has been marginalised and by marginalising her you also marginalise your readership base. Lord knows she's not an easy person to live with and many have been toe to toe with Margo, but ... constantly pissing in the readers' faces is not a way to ensure a long term future.'

Fairfax and the government were not the only ones applying pressure. ABC management told Phillip Adams to drop Kingston's regular 'Canberra Babylon' piece from his show. When Adams refused, the ABC told him that at the very least he had to include someone else who would 'balance' Kingston. Eventually he was forced to end the segment on the grounds that Kingston was no longer based in the national capital and that therefore there was no longer a 'Canberra' in Canberra Babylon.

To add to her problems, Kingston's health was deteriorating. She had for years nursed a chronic back problem, and this was getting worse. *Webdiary* was taking more and more of her time, especially dealing with the comments. Then, during the 2004 election campaign, Fairfax decided to close *Webdiary*.

Naturally, Kingston wanted to keep the site open, and she asked management how that might be possible. They told her that they were willing to allow her to take a 'seachange' package, an arrangement that would become common a decade later as Australia's newspapers cut staff in the wake of falling revenues. Essentially, this meant that she went onto a contract at a greatly reduced wage and was more or less restricted to work on *Webdiary*, something she was willing to do to save the site. One bright spot in all this was that management also offered to install a comments system, which everyone thought would make it easier to deal with reader correspondence. 'Famous last words!' Kingston told me in our interview.

Comments flooded in. In a way that would become familiar to those involved in online media well into the future, including to me when I was running a blog for News Limited, the moderation of comments became the most taxing and time-consuming part of the job. 'It just got completely out of control,' Kingston explained. At one point, she actually used her own money to employ someone to help her, but this was clearly not a long-term solution.

So, in the tradition of the approach that was her hallmark at *Webdiary*, she asked her readers if they had any suggestions. She was inundated with offers.

Kingston sighed as she recounted this. 'We put a proposal to Fairfax that the community would run it and manage it and we would just contract *Webdiary* to them [Fairfax]. It made sense. It actually saved them money, and the online people at Fairfax said yes, but then it was no from senior management. I finally got jack of it.'

But it wasn't quite over yet. In early 2005, management sent her a memo saying that they thought *Webdiary* was too much work for her and they had a plan to help. They would introduce a new raft of bloggers, using software that would be uniform for all of them, and they would employ moderators to handle the comments. There were some conditions, however. The code of ethics Kingston had developed for *Webdiary* had to go. Equally galling, the regular contributions she published from among her readers would no longer be accepted. This violated the interactive nature of what *Webdiary* had become, especially as Kingston felt that part of her success had been in nurturing new writing talent. 'I used to say to my editor and others at the *Herald*, "Look, I'm actually developing a stable of extremely talented writers; why don't we select a piece I like, or the paper likes, and publish it in the paper?" They just thought that was ridiculous.'

The biggest change was that Kingston would no longer be able to post directly to *Webdiary*. Everything she wrote, under this new proposal, would have to go through a vetting process.

Stephen Hutcheon later explained that there was nothing unusual in this. 'These days, it's difficult to do that because so many people are filing or tweeting or posting at any given moment. Back then, the velocity of new material hitting the website between major updates was relatively small and such editorial oversight was possible.

'Anyway, she didn't observe that instruction. I went into her post to edit something she had written — as was my right — and that was the end of a beautiful experiment that was ahead of its time. She pulled the pin and went indy.'

Kingston's departure ended the first full-scale attempt by a mainstream Australian media organisation to come to terms with the disruptions caused by the new online technology. And as tempting as it is to view it as a noble experiment that didn't quite get off the ground, I think we have to be careful not to impose in hindsight a shape and intention that was never really there. It is a teachable moment in the history of Australian media — it was certainly an important development — but it was also an idiosyncratic experiment.

As Stephen Hutcheon put it to me, 'Based on what we know now, I think you can describe it as a trailblazer. I'm particularly proud of many things we did. Not the least was the Grass Roots project during one federal election, where we worked with large groups of students from UTS to file stories from their own electorates about local issues. That was awesome. And difficult. And a bit patchy. But it was innovative.

'I think Margo was unique in terms of her passion, and the rest was just happenstance — the right place, the right time, the right person, the right boss.'

I asked him if he thought that it was a missed opportunity for Fairfax, that they might've had their own *Huffington Post* on their hands, and he said, 'There were lots of lost opportunities in the early 2000s. That said, Fairfax did continue to develop its online operations as a separate business, insulated from print. Perhaps *Webdiary* could have become a HuffPo, but that's with the benefit of hindsight.'

The story of *Webdiary* cannot be separated from the personality of Margo Kingston. It was as much about Kingston's relationship with the management at Fairfax as it was about anything intrinsic to online media. Fairfax made mistakes. A braver, less conservative organisation might have found a way to make it work. At various points in the process, they did attempt to accommodate this brave new world that was evolving right before their eyes, but ultimately they weren't up to the challenge. Stephen Hutcheon told me that 'there wasn't much appreciation at the time about the trailblazing role [Kingston] was setting in what we now know as crowdsourcing, social media and community engagement. We're talking about the early 2000s and Big Media still thought it was bullet-proof from digital disruption'.

Whatever you think about Kingston's work and what finally happened to her, she was 15 years ahead of virtually everyone else in Australian journalism. As the debates continue throughout the world about the future of the profession, as hands are wrung and oracles — I mean social-media experts — are consulted, few are saying anything more than what Margo Kingston was saying, and practising, at *Webdiary*. She made mistakes — of course she did. She nonetheless figured out some key answers years before anyone else was asking the questions. She deserves enormous respect for that.

Kingston was a gatekeeper who considered it her job to let uncredentialled, unknown, unfamous, ordinary citizens in on the national conversation, rather than to lock them out. To this day, there is no one in the Australian mainstream media who has been willing to play that role to the same extent.

*Webdiary* was my introduction to new media and it gave me some practical experience in the sort of discussions about democracy, citizenship, and public debate I was theorising about in my PhD. I didn't realise it at the time, but it also made me better able to understand the potential of blogging when I first stumbled across it.

## CHAPTER TWO

# *On* The Road to Surfdom

*Once it [the war in Iraq] is behind us, the whole world will benefit*
*from cheaper oil, which will be a bigger stimulus than anything else.*
RUPERT MURDOCH, NEWS CORP. CEO

In December 2001, my family and I moved to the United
States. It was the first time I had been to the self-styled
land of the brave and home of the free, and it was a hell of a
time to be there. The country was still raw from the attacks
of September 11, and in my neighbourhood in Washington,
DC, cars, front doors, and lawns were decorated with
American flags, and sometimes far less subtle assertions of
national pride and defiance. I saw bumper stickers that said
things like, 'America: love it or leave it.' There were posters
of gun-toting cartoon eagles laying waste to rooms full of
'ragheads'. The nation had embraced George W. Bush with
stellar approval ratings. He had already committed troops
to Afghanistan, as had John Howard.

Once we were settled in, I started to consume the local
media like the interested visitor from a fellow democratic
nation I was. I arranged to have *The Washington Post* and

*The New York Times* home delivered. I started watching Fox News and all the other cable channels that were available, and I listened to Rush Limbaugh and Sean Hannity on the radio in the afternoons. The intensity of the rhetoric, especially on talk radio, was kind of amazing, and among it all, not a word of criticism for the president. It was easy to believe then that America really was the *United* States, that there was a unanimity of opinion brought about by the 9/11 attacks that would hold indefinitely. All the other divisions that were likely to be normal in a country of 300 million people seemed to have been voluntarily subsumed in the name of recovering from the terror that had rained down upon them.

But soon enough, even during our first weeks in the country, there were hints that all was not as harmonious as the media coverage suggested. About a month after we moved in, in late January 2002, there was a knock at the door, and we opened it to find a woman with a bottle of wine in her hand.

'Hello,' she said, with a lovely American drawl. 'I'm your neighbour, Katherine. I'm sorry I haven't been in earlier to welcome you to the neighbourhood. I brought you this,' she said, and offered us the wine. 'And I just really wanted to apologise about our president.'

I was stunned. Her words so jarred with the general impression I had formed of the mood of the country that I half-expected the patriotism police to drop from the sky and arrest us. It went through my mind that she was joking, but by the time we'd sat down with her and finished the wine, I was completely cured of my narrow view of local public opinion.

Maybe Katherine's unexpected criticism of President Bush emboldened me. We had rented a house in north-west Washington, DC, as lovely a suburban neighbourhood as you are likely to find in any country in the world. The area stood in stark contrast to other parts of DC, a place where you could move from the comfortable, reasonably safe middle class to the extremes of first-world poverty and violence by crossing a single street on your way to the south-east of the city. Among the sea of flags in the neighbourhood, there was even one stuck to the wall beside the front door of our rented house. It was only little, about one foot by six inches, and we were happy for it to be there. Still, given that we weren't American, it felt odd, almost like false advertising. While I had no intention of taking it down, I did want some way of showing that we weren't from around there. So after some searching, I managed to track down an Australian flag of the same size, and we affixed it to the wall directly below the US one. It was a respectful way of identifying ourselves as outsiders without offering offence to the locals.

What happened next was almost surreal. As I walked around the suburb over the next few weeks, either going to the shops or taking my son to school, I noticed something. The house at the end of our street, which had a full-size flagpole in the front lawn and an American flag permanently upon it, now also flew a Spanish flag underneath. Further along, the pole affixed to the front of another house, on which the American flag also fluttered, had been joined by a new pole proudly displaying the Greek flag. Elsewhere, an Italian flag and a Union Jack appeared alongside star-spangled banners, and I even saw an Icelandic flag a few blocks away. Inadvertently, our small act of national identification had triggered a subtle blossoming of patriotic differentiation across the neighbourhood. The diversity that was hidden beneath the quotidian surface slowly revealed itself, and the solidarity presented in the media as a simple fact was exposed as more complex.

But it wasn't until I immersed myself in the growing world of online discussion that I really understood just how deceptive — and actively so — that media image of unquestioned support for President Bush actually was. Soon I was online a lot, beginning to get a sense of the texture of this infinite landscape of information. It was exciting, and I had some sense that we were on the verge of something new in the way we communicated with each other about matters of social importance, but it was a vague and confusing feeling. I was in a kind of suspended awe, in the way that those who see the ocean sucked out from the beach before a tsunami must be.

Before leaving Australia, I had submitted my thesis on the role of intellectuals in public debate. It was really a discussion of citizenship, and over the course of the four years I spent researching and writing it, I looked at the relationship between experts and ordinary citizens, between those who devise and implement policy and the rest of us, the general population whose role in determining the running of the country was more and more reduced to statistical averages garnered from opinion polls and focus groups. Yes, we got to vote, but in between times we were pretty much expected to shut up and leave everything to our betters. The great disconnect in our democratic society, it seemed, was the gap between those with expertise in all the many and various skills needed to run a successful country, and the rest of the population, the lay citizenry, the ordinary people of the cities and the suburbs. This was largely a power divide, and it served to render an elite as active participants in the life of the nation and the rest of us as passive observers. Absent the authority and prestige that comes from a recognised qualification or experience in a given field, how exactly were 'ordinary people' meant to contribute to public debate? And given their lack of expertise, why exactly did it matter if they didn't?

It seemed to me at the time that there was a pervasive view within elite circles, including the media, that the 'general public' just weren't up to the task of participation, that they lacked the skills and knowledge necessary to participate effectively in the decision-making process, and that therefore they should be excluded from all such activities. Comments such as those made more recently by senior ABC reporter Marius Benson were pretty typical at the time. In an article on the ABC website titled 'Dumbing

Down Politics: the problem is you', Benson wrote, 'The real problem is not the media, not the politicians; it is you — you the voter. The level of knowledge that lies behind the average vote is distressingly slight.'

He continued:

Before the last election I had many conversations with voters. One was with a local shopkeeper. Having handed over the bread and yoghurt he launched into his analysis of the election ahead.

'They're going to put up the GST to 20%, for sure. Doesn't matter who wins, they'll both do it — 20% minimum.' He saw that fantasy as the central truth at stake in the election.

Other conversations were with professional people, people earning six and seven figure sums — five times as much as an average backbencher and more. They had a clear view on how they were going to vote, a view based on inherited beliefs combined with a near complete ignorance of current issues.

… Faced with this level of indifference and ignorance what are politicians meant to do beyond picking three slogans, repeating them endlessly and hoping something will get through to people who only hear them accidentally when they tune in too early for *MasterChef* and catch a political grab on the news headlines?

The contempt these comments displayed for the writer's fellow citizens was disturbing enough. The fact that they came from a person whose job it is to inform the public, and therefore likely to be one of those responsible, at least in part, for the level of ignorance he presumed to be so appalled by, betrayed an almost comical lack of self-awareness.

Traditionally, citizens who wanted to involve themselves in political discussions, especially in Australia, might have joined a political party or a trade union. Both of these institutions provided a way for the 'grassroots' to participate in serious discussion of social and political matters, and to hone their knowledge in a way that enabled them to participate meaningfully in the civic life of the nation. And indeed, both these paths are still available, though it is fair to say neither institution really fulfils that role anymore. (Perhaps the smaller parties like the Greens and those others that spring up from time to time in response to the dominance of the two major parties do, but their effect is limited, while major party and union memberships are a fraction of what they were even 20 years ago.) So how else might people participate?

In my thesis I examined an interesting possibility that had been imported to Australia from the United States at around the time that Australia was debating becoming a republic: deliberative polling. A polling company selected a representative sample of around 300 citizens; these citizens were invited to a weekend of discussion on the topic of whether Australia should become a republic. Those who accepted the invitation were given information kits on the pros and cons of the argument. They were flown to Canberra and provided with accommodation, and for two days were immersed in the arguments for and against a republic. They were able to break into smaller groups and discuss what they had heard and formulate questions to ask experts. Both at the beginning and at the end of the two-day public debate, the participants were polled on whether they wanted Australia to become a republic, and the vote in favour rose considerably. The whole two-day confab was telecast by ABC Television, and if you watched it you would have seen a bunch of ordinary people go from being passive and intimidated civic supplicants to being active participants, empowered by their involvement in a meaningful public debate.

Still, deliberative polling, I concluded, was hardly a panacea. It was expensive and perhaps subject to becoming something of a long-term novelty. I suggested that we could incorporate a similar process into the committee system of one or both houses of parliament — though it would be a bit like turning up the music because the vacuum cleaner was too loud. The easier and smarter thing to do was to turn off the vacuum cleaner; it was better to have citizens involved in the democratic process earlier, rather than trying to concoct systems that wedged them into it sometime later.

What we needed, I rather wistfully concluded, was some sort of forum where experts and ordinary citizens could discuss matters of democratic importance as civic equals.

I submitted the thesis in November 2001. Then I went to America and read my first blog.

This was my very own God-particle moment. Just as physicists had shown theoretically that the Higgs boson existed but lacked the tools to actually see one, my thesis had theorised a democratic space that blogs now made visible.

As is hardly surprising, given that I'd just spent four years researching various forms of public debate, I saw the potential of blogging immediately, and I may well have gone overboard in talking it up. I was temporarily that awful thing, a cyber enthusiast. But it wasn't only me; blogs were creating excitement among people all over the world, who suddenly found that they were no longer just an audience for media but genuine contributors to it. I wrote in an essay at the time:

A blogger is somebody who writes a weblog. A weblog is a website where a person logs, often on a daily basis, his or her thoughts on a range of topics ... Once you have your site, it is available for all and sundry to see and, if you wish, you can set it up so that readers can leave comments about individual posts. There are now a large number of reasonably well-established weblogs that attract anywhere up to several hundred thousand readers a week each, and though this is small potatoes compared to mainstream networks and traditional media it does represent something of a phenomenon.

To some people, weblogs (*blogs*, as the word is almost universally abbreviated to) are a geek hula-hoop, a fad that will pass once the novelty wears off, a bit of fun, but not something to get too excited about. To others they represent a rebirth of participatory democracy, a new form of journalism, and even the home of the new public intellectuals.

The discovery of blogging meant that citizenship had just become much more interesting, and those of us close to the ground floor of this brave new world were right to be excited. Religious extremists had just flown jetliners into tall buildings and killed thousands of people. The West had launched a war in Afghanistan and was already hinting at one in Iraq. If that moment wasn't the right time to hear from the citizenry at large, then I don't know when was. And the sheer numbers who began blogging around this time indicated that the people wanted to be heard.

Because of course, that sense of unanimity in US society didn't last long. Had the war in Afghanistan finished quickly and successfully, perhaps the United States would have coped and moved on. Maybe if Osama bin Laden had been captured or killed in those early days, there would have been a feeling of justice served and, to use that distinctively American word, a sense of closure. But none of that happened, and the lack of resolution, which is still playing itself out in American politics to this day, fed the soil from which a million blogs bloomed.

In November 2000, George W. Bush had been elected president in a controversial election that was ultimately decided by partisan lawyers sitting on the Supreme Court. The Twin Towers had come down on 11 September 2001. The United States, with the support of Australia, had invaded Afghanistan on 7 October 2001. On 20 December, 100 days after the 9/11 attacks, the fires at Ground Zero were officially declared out by the New York City Fire Department, and 100 days after that, those in power were already talking publicly about the 'need' to invade Iraq. People were in shock. People were angry. Politicians, from George W. Bush to Tony Blair to John Howard, were not only trying to figure out what to do to keep us safe, but also how to use what had happened to bolster their political standing. Everything seemed to contribute to the sense of foreboding, whether it was the white powder being mailed to US newsrooms and offices on Capitol Hill, or the killing spree launched by the so-called Washington Sniper. Never in my lifetime had we more needed a level-headed, trustworthy media able to live up to its own hype about being the fourth estate. Never in my lifetime were more ordinary people paying such close attention to what the fourth estate was doing. More importantly, never before had so many ordinary people had the tools to fact-check the priesthood of the fourth estate. It's little wonder a good bit of defrocking was to go on.

Former publisher of *The New York Times* Arthur Sulzberger once said, 'You're not buying news when you buy *The New York Times*. You're buying judgment.' He was exactly right, and it did not only apply to *The New York Times*. Judgement was the basis of all journalistic authority, and in the wake of September 11 it was found wanting.

I think many of us who started writing and reading blogs around this time — and the blogosphere was a joint project between writers *and* readers — were under no illusions about the shortcomings of the media. We understood that it revelled in sensationalism, that it was swayed by the demands of its advertisers, and that some publishers and owners were not averse to using their media properties to push their commercial interests in other areas. But until we started to write our own analyses and pay the close attention that blogging demands, I don't think many of us quite realised the extent to which 'the news' was something that was constructed from the ground up, rather than a reflection of a pre-existing reality. Journalists weren't just the messengers — they were the message. It wasn't only that we discovered that they sometimes got their facts wrong or put a political spin on allegedly neutral information, or that they saw things differently from us. It was the realisation that by its very nature journalism constructs a version of reality, and that the accuracy of that version can be impeded by the structures and habits of the profession itself.

Yet there is a risk in looking back to those early days of political blogging with rose-coloured glasses and suggesting that blogs were some sort of utopia of deliberative democracy, and I want to avoid that here. As fondly as I remember those early days, the truth is, everything that was good and bad about blogging was present from the start.

*The Road to Surfdom* went live in May 2002. The archives of my earliest attempts at blogging are far from complete, but I can tell you that I used the free blogger.com platform, which was the basis of the blogging revolution that was well underway by 2002. I used the name *The Road to Surfdom* from the beginning, but I remember thinking it didn't matter much what I called it as it was unlikely to last very long anyway, and no one outside a handful of friends was ever likely to read it. I can absolutely promise you that the thought never crossed my mind that what I was doing had anything to do with journalism.

There were other issues to negotiate. A reasonable number of the blogs I was reading had anonymous authors, and I did consider disappearing behind a pseudonym. I'm far from anti-social, but I do tend very strongly to the shy end of the spectrum, so it was tempting to conceal my identity. But shy as I may be, I was also enough of an egotist to want to see my name in lights — even the tiny, dim lights of a new blog. More importantly, I believed that if you were going to express political opinions you should do so under your own name. I'd already had the experience on *Webdiary* of being attacked by people who used pseudonyms, and it struck me as pretty unsatisfactory. I wouldn't have said such people were gutless, exactly, but I thought that you should be allowed to face your accuser and that critics owed it to you to not pretend they were someone else. So I sucked up my misgivings and dismissed the idea of anonymity.

Anonymity is, of course, still an issue in the ongoing negotiation of the rules and conventions that govern the public space provided by social media. I must say, though, that I've changed my mind on it. There are legitimate reasons for people not using their real names, not least that they often lack the institutional support that many of those who call them cowards take for granted. It is relatively easy to voice strong opinions when you know you have the backing of a political party or a trade union, a business council, or even a media organisation. It's a lot harder to enter those discussions when you are simply a citizen, a stray and inexperienced voice in a largely professionalised space. Anonymity is about the only thing you can use to armour yourself. Most of the objections to anonymity are motivated by a desire to keep ordinary people away from public debate, part of a broader process of demonisation and deterrence that arises whenever citizens try to play a role in their own democracy. I chose from the beginning to use my own name and I've never regretted the decision, although it doesn't mean I haven't sometimes wished I'd made a different choice.

Another thing I remember from the early days of *Surfdom* is spending an embarrassingly long time trying to figure out some of the technicalities of my new website. As easy to use as Blogger was, I quickly discovered that there were some bells and whistles you could add if you could just figure out how to do it. One was permalinks, pieces of code that give each individual post on a blog a unique URL, so you could link to a specific post and not just to the front page of the blog. Another was a hit counter, which allowed you to see not only how many people had found their way to your site, but also where they were coming from: whether a reader had stumbled across you via Google or had followed a link from another blog. Counters were important because without a metric for measuring traffic you had absolutely no sense of your blog as part of a network: you were untethered in a vast, dark ocean. With a hit counter and its associated statistics, the stars suddenly came out, and you could learn to navigate by them. I also added a blogroll, which, in those early days, was the chief marketing tool a blogger had. People really paid attention to them, and if your blog happened to be listed by a high-profile blog, it was not only a badge of honour; it drove traffic. I noticed this when journalist Eric Alterman listed *Surfdom* on his carefully curated blogroll on the MSNBC site and I was suddenly getting a thousand extra hits a month.

All of these innovations now come as standard in most blogging packages. Back then, such code was supplied by third parties. This meant, God help the amateur, that you had to learn how to open up the backend of your blog and insert the relevant code. If you put it in the wrong place, you could destroy the whole site, or at least render it incoherent, and let's just say the early versions of *Surfdom* were lucky to survive my coding 'skills'. Eventually I was fortunate enough to have a reader by the name of Neale Talbot take pity on me. To this day, my gratitude knows no bounds.

My earliest posts on *The Road to Surfdom* tended to be observations about living in the United States, or else drew on the stuff I had written about in my thesis. (Believe me, after being immersed in the thing for the previous four years, it was pretty difficult to get it out of my head!) From the beginning, I was obsessed with accessibility, aware of writing for a general audience, and I tried to avoid the sort of deadening prose for which academics are famous; though by the same token, I'm sure not too many people would've found the stuff I was writing particularly riveting. Early on, Gareth Parker, a young blogger based in Perth (who later gave up blogging and became a full-time journalist), responded to one of my posts by saying it was way too long; I would have to learn that blogging was about short, sharp posts, not essays. I responded by saying something like, it's my blog and I'll blog how I want to, and surely that was the beauty of the form, that people could make of it what they would. He in turn responded, graciously, that I'd made a good point. It sounds anodyne, but to me it exemplified the sort of reasoned exchange that was possible with blogging. Where in the 'old' media could such an exchange happen, let alone in real time? It is also a good illustration of how conscious we all were that we were inventing a new form.

Still, it wasn't long before the partisan nature of blogging became apparent. One of my early posts attracted the ire of Tim Blair. Tim was a journalist based in Sydney and, to his eternal credit, was one of the first professionals in Australia to realise the potential of new media. He took a completely different approach to the matter, but in his own way he was as much an online pioneer as Margo Kingston. Over time, his blog would become closely aligned with the right wing of the US blogosphere, and it would prove incredibly popular. His attack on my post was something of a shock. It wasn't just that it was abusive, but that it didn't engage with what I'd said. I was genuinely surprised that someone would attack something just for the sake of it. What a naïf I was.

I emailed Tim to say that he could've at least read what I said before attacking it.

He wrote back: 'Welcome to the blogosphere!'

For Tim, blogs were less a place for measured deliberation than an arena for political battle, and that was how he ran his. This was a valid choice, but what I found interesting was that it was a professional journalist who took this position. Tim was hardly alone in doing it, and certainly I gave as good as I got on many occasions. But given the amount of hand-wringing that is done these days about the appalling standards of online discussion, it is worth remembering that the professionals were just as culpable in establishing this trend as we amateur bloggers. In fact, there is a pretty solid argument that says they were more influential, given that they were professionals and thus had the endorsement of institutions with genuine standing in our society. The likes of Rush Limbaugh, Ann Coulter, and Sean Hannity were already being paid millions to be abusive on air, and they were doing it in prime time; journalists who blogged with vitriol were simply following their example. Fox News was, and is, the gold standard for propaganda passing itself off as journalism, and it has done more to create the post-truth environment that now infects much political debate than any number of amateur bloggers could ever have dreamed of doing.

But the problem goes deeper than one network. Unchallenged until recently in its ability to shape public debate, the mainstream media has fallen into bad habits. These have not only distorted debate, but have also made journalists reluctant to listen to criticism. Jay Rosen, a professor of journalism at New York University, has a word that he uses to describe a particular sort of journalism — or rather, a particular attitude adopted by many journalists — and it is useful here: 'savviness'. Savviness is a kind of smug knowingness, an attitude that professes to have a dispassionate and practical understanding of how politics 'really' works, a frame of mind allegedly available only to those on the inside. It is not the same as objectivity, and it certainly has nothing to do with analysis. It isn't quite cynicism, though it easily slips over into it. Rosen captures its cloying self-satisfaction when he describes its practitioners as being the 'church of the savvy', as if they were members of a cult. He writes on his blog:

[I]n order for this belief system to operate effectively, it has to continually position the journalist and his or her observations not as right where others are wrong, or virtuous where others are corrupt, or visionary where others are short-sighted, but as practical, hardheaded, unsentimental, and shrewd where others are didactic, ideological, and dreamy.

Savviness leads to all sorts of complications, a veritable body of practice that ultimately renders journalists ineffective at keeping the public properly informed. It leads to the sort of faux objectivity called 'balance', where the views of both sides are given equal weight, regardless of their intellectual worth. It leads to 'he said/she said' journalism, in which journalistic judgement is replaced by rote quote-matching. It drains political discussion of any overt acknowledgement of the way power works, and thus robs political debate of politics itself.

Savviness creates the conditions of journalism's demise, which is where blogging comes in.

Sure, the media industry has been in trouble for over a decade because the internet has undermined its ability to make money by destroying its monopoly on classified advertising, while also rendering display ads less lucrative. But the media's problem is not merely technological disruption and a broken business model. Its problem is that it began to take itself so seriously that it failed to notice, or care, that nobody else did. Savviness was at once both rationalisation and armour. By trying so hard to assert its own authority over material that was properly the possession of every citizen in the land — the news — it robbed democracy of its citizens. Media outlets became gatekeepers who thought they had the right to sanction who got to speak in public, and today they are still trying to recover from the fact that the new tools of social media, beginning with blogging, allow ordinary people to route around them.

Blogging was the opposite of savviness. We were not insiders. We were not trying to assert our professional access to proprietary information and burnish our credentials by sharing it. We were not trying to justify a salary by pretending to be better informed than we were. We saw no particular reason to come across as definitive. We didn't seek to assert our authority, only our ability to participate in a conversation; even those of us who had some sort of specialist knowledge didn't feel the need to have the final say. We were talking to, not at, our audience.

Crucial to the cult of savviness is journalists' understanding of who their audience is. There is a very real sense in which journalists, particularly political journalists, aren't actually writing for their customers. A lot of political journalism is designed not so much to impart information to an audience of ordinary people as to signal membership of the cult of the savvy to fellow members. In other words, it is written to be read by other journalists or the politicians themselves, or by that small strata of professionals — staffers, public servants, lobbyists, consultants — who move in the same limited circles. To the extent that the audience is considered at all, it is to co-opt them into this inner circle, to make them feel like they, too, are on the inside.

But who did bloggers imagine they were talking to? At first we were talking to each other, to other bloggers. In those early days, blogs didn't take comments. So when people talked about the 'blogosphere', they meant a series of blogs that linked to one another, run by writers who conversed via their posts: if you read something on a blog that you wanted to comment on, you wrote about it on your own blog, and hoped that by linking to the original piece you would send your readers to that source. You then hoped that the other bloggers would check their counter and see that there were new readers coming to their blog from yours and that they would link back to your piece and thus send some of their readers to your blog.

As a new form of communication, blogging very quickly developed its own rules and its own grammar, and, although its boundaries were pretty generous, most of those who were successful at it internalised a common idea of what a blog was supposed to be. They also worked hard. A successful blog was one that updated regularly, and the time and effort required to do that was enormous. The image of some unemployed loser in his mother's basement incoherently railing against the perceived evils of the world is still one that is conjured up today, but it was always a caricature. In fact, I'd go so far as to say that the mainstream media, particularly in Australia, deliberately cultivated it in order to discredit what they — misleadingly — saw as their competition. Many of the earliest bloggers were in fact professionals: people from universities, or practising lawyers or economists who devoted their spare time to blogging, reflecting on the issues of the day and bringing to bear their own specialist knowledge and experience. Many were simply regular citizens, people with a point of view who, prior to the existence of the technology, had no easy way of entering the discussion. It is important to realise that this sort of writing, this sort of participation in public debate, was undertaken by people with serious intent, regardless of political affiliation. It wasn't always pretty, and it often offended those with traditional notions of how such discussions should take place, but it was rarely the ill-disciplined rantfest that its critics liked to pretend it was. As robust as some of the discussion on blogs could and can be, the scandal is not that participants were sometimes rude to each other but that, until blogging was invented, such people were effectively blocked from public debate.

There was also an incredible feeling of collegiality among most in the blogosphere. If you liked someone's blog, you emailed and told them so, and when they linked to your site, you wrote and thanked them. I got to know some great people this way, and eventually met some of them in person. I'm still in contact with many of them, more than a decade later. The blogosphere is vast — even in 2002 it was — but it can feel personal and manageable.

It's the same dynamic that now attracts millions of people to Facebook or Twitter or other social-media sites. It is silly to dismiss it as somehow less real just because it happens in a virtual space.

As blogs multiplied, the technology became more sophisticated. Comments boxes, in particular, changed things considerably. They introduced a closer relationship between the individual blogger and his or her audience, as well as between the readers themselves. They also created a subtle but undeniable pressure to change how you related to other blogs. The combination of having a comments box and a hit counter — metrics for how 'popular' you were — put you in direct competition with other blogs. Whereas in the earliest days most bloggers had been meticulous in acknowledging where they got their information from by linking to it, as time went on there was a temptation to bypass the originating blog and link to the source material as if you had come across it independently. The idea behind this was that if you were seen as the 'source' for a particular story, other blogs would cite you as such, and thus drive traffic your way. All of this went to reputation. It was the blogging equivalent of a 'scoop', even if it just meant you happened to be the first one to mention something you'd found in the mainstream media. If this sounds petty, it was, but it is hard to overstate how addictive traffic was. In the absence of other remuneration, traffic became a money substitute, a form of display that signalled your place in a pecking order. It was a way of justifying to yourself the hours you spent writing the stuff for no financial return. It had its ignoble side, but an obsession with hits was probably something of a psychological necessity.

But notice what else this says about the medium. Implicit in all of this is the idea that what we wrote about on blogs was what others were saying. Specifically, what we wrote about was what those in the mainstream media were saying. Journalists often latched onto this fact as proof of their own primacy and of the basically sycophantic relationship blogs had with the 'real' media, and there is some truth in that. The mistake journalists made, though, was to conclude from this unexceptional fact that what bloggers were doing was therefore second-rate or somehow unworthy, that it was 'unoriginal' and added nothing new to the conversation. To jump to that conclusion was to miss — or to be in denial about — what was really happening. It was not only to make a category error, but also to misunderstand the changing relationship between the media and its audience. Blogs weren't just adding to the conversation; they were creating a conversation where none had previously existed. While journalists were cultivating backroom sources and other anonymous leads, we were cultivating an audience.

Blogging was not a species of journalism; it was a species of citizenship. We weren't trying to report; we were trying to understand or simply to express an opinion. In doing so, we talked to each other — to as many as wanted to join in — about what was dominating public discussion.

We became not only the most attentive audience the mainstream media had ever had, but also its sharpest critics. And many journalists never forgave us.

In one sense, blogs were to the mainstream media what 1960s British rock was to black music from the Mississippi Delta: we riffed on what we found in the big newspapers and on the cable and network channels, just as Eric Clapton and Led Zeppelin riffed on Robert Johnson and Son House. Yes, it was a kind of appropriation, but it also changed the material and added value to it, re-presented it in a way that made sense to an audience that was largely being ignored by the mainstream itself.

There was nothing particularly new about this sort of re-presentation: radio and television had been appropriating the journalism produced by newspapers from the moment they came into existence, and it is well understood in the industry that the newspaper is the engine room of much journalistic output. This is precisely why Rupert Murdoch owns newspapers, because he understands that they set the agenda for the media more generally and thus are a source of power and influence. Blogs, in that sense, were just another platform relying on the spadework done by newspapers.

But there was more to it than this. In 'appropriating' content from the mainstream we weren't seeking to set ourselves up as competition to the profession; we were merely taking for granted the primacy of the media as source and site for ongoing public discussion, and we were trying to muscle our way into that conversation. Much to our surprise, we found an audience for what we were saying. A big one.

I was lucky I started blogging in the United States. The practice took hold in America much more decisively than it did in Australia, and therefore I was swept up in a much bigger *thing* than I would've been had I started at home. But there was a qualitative difference, too. The numbers you sensed around you had a pleasant coddling effect. I felt oddly protected in a public sphere that size, faceless yet empowered, invisible yet present — a phenomenon that has been noticed by country kids moving to the big city for eons. If the crowd is big enough, even a nobody can feel he or she is in the middle of something.

There is also something liberating about speaking your mind when you are a long way from home. I don't buy the argument that distance gives you perspective — the sort of logic that has blinded expats such as Germaine Greer and Robert Hughes to the shortcomings of their critiques of Australia — but you do feel less beholden to the niceties of your upbringing, and that's not a bad thing when you are trying to argue in public. You feel less like you have someone looking over your shoulder. Even now, living back in Australia, I sometimes hanker for that feeling.

Once blogging became dominated by discussion of the war in Iraq and surrounding issues, it was good being an Australian in America for other reasons, too.

To American readers, it was interesting to come across a foreign perspective on events in their own country, while to Australian readers it was novel to have a local in the middle of the action. As a reader once said to me, *Surfdom* was like the Australian blogosphere's own foreign correspondent.

Don't forget, though, that this was all happening at a particular moment in time, and that influenced the way things unfolded.

As the war continued, blogs such as *Instapundit*, *Daily Kos*, and *Eschaton*, and bloggers such as Kevin Drum, Matt Yglesias, Tim Blair, Josh Marshall, and Digby started attracting significant audiences. *Surfdom* was swept up in the excitement, and although it never reached the top-tier status of those just mentioned, it was nonetheless receiving significant traffic. It seemed that people had found in the blogosphere voices that were offering an alternative view, one that dared question the version of events being offered by the mainstream. Yes, the discussion was politicised, but of course it was: we were discussing politics! The difference was that we had no need to assume the faux objectivity that the church of the savvy considered essential. We just said what we thought. This led, inevitably, to the odd slanging match between the left and the right, but it would be wrong to say — and it is often still said — that the blogosphere, and social media more generally, created polarisation in the public arena. It didn't; it just reflected it, and there was a certain integrity in this. No one was under any illusions as to where various bloggers stood.

When the Bush administration and its acolyte governments in the United Kingdom and Australia began making the case for an invasion of Iraq based on Saddam Hussein's alleged possession of weapons of mass destruction, and then maintained the fiction in the face of all evidence to the contrary, standard journalistic techniques lulled the professionals into error. *The New York Times* in particular, through its senior reporter Judith Miller, fell hook, line, and sinker for the lies of an anonymous source — the man nicknamed Curveball — and reported with practised authority information that was wrong, and for which they later, partially, apologised.

Part of the failure was political: for all their protestations about objectivity and neutrality, much of the media is affected by a slant to either the left or the right. As ex-Murdoch employee Andrew Neil, a former editor of *The Sunday Times*, told a parliamentary inquiry in Britain, '[T]he Murdoch empire was more united on Iraq than the Bush administration.' That is to say, not one of Mr Murdoch's papers anywhere in the world editorialised against the invasion of Iraq. But the bigger problem was institutional, rather than anything to do with bias per se. Much of the mainstream had become, well, *mainstream*, to the point that they identified with other sources of power in society, including the government, rather than acting as a watchdog over them. This identification happened regardless of the ostensible slant of the media organisation itself. Former *New York Times* foreign correspondent Daniel Simpson has said of his then employer: 'It seemed pretty glaringly obvious to me that the "news fit to print" was pretty much the news that's fit to serve the powerful. The way that the paper's senior staff think is exactly like those in power — in fact, it's their job to become their friends.' He noted that his bosses were 'looking for every possible way of getting this weapons-of-mass-destruction story into the news media', and that he 'came under enormous pressure … to start looking at it the same way'; that is, to report bogus information that supported the idea that Saddam had weapons of mass destruction. Similarly, academic Robert Manne, in his 2011 *Quarterly Essay*, said of *The Australian* newspaper that it

> played the role not so much of reporter or interpreter but rather of national enforcer of those values that lie at the heart of the Murdoch empire: market fundamentalism and the beneficence of American global hegemony. Unquestioning support for American foreign policy led it to the conduct of an extraordinarily strident campaign in favour of an invasion that was launched on the basis of false intelligence, that has been responsible for perhaps 400,000 deaths, and for which it has never uttered a word of apology.

Why wasn't the blogosphere fooled? Well, in truth, parts of it were, especially the part of it that leaned right and that wanted to act as a support for the Bush administration.

But opposition to the war, and credulity about the administration's case for it, did not cleave necessarily to the standard left/right divide. The more compelling divide was between those who were willing to follow the evidence and note the naked emperor, and those who weren't.

But how could a bunch of amateurs possibly be better informed than an industry of professionals and all their contacts? This is where the internet came into its own. There was evidence out there, and blogs were able to marshal it in a compelling way. Whether it was experts on the Middle East such as Juan Cole starting their own blogs and sharing their knowledge or the simple fact that key documents were now available online, the net effect was that the mainstream media no longer had proprietorial control over information. We could all access the UN website and read the reports from various weapons inspectors, or we could go to a university website and read what different experts had said about a given issue. I spent hours on the White House website and that of Prime Minister Howard, reading the transcripts of speeches and interviews, and offering alternative views of what they all meant, comparing what was said with facts on the record, or with comments made at other times. Sometimes it was as simple as being able to read a book and quote relevant sections; one of the most successful series of posts I ever published was a rolling review of a book by former national security adviser Richard Clarke. By simply writing about each chapter as I read it, I cultivated a huge readership of people who were curious to know what Clarke had said. This series of posts was linked to by hundreds of other blogs. Technology liberated a whole stratum of engaged citizens from a reliance upon old media and allowed us to engage with other citizens in genuinely meaningful and informative ways.

Nothing was stopping the mainstream media from using the same sources, of course, but the church of the savvy tended to put more faith in their insider, anonymous sources than the sort of documents that good bloggers relied on. As Paul Krugman noted on his blog:

> A lot of political journalism, and even reporting on policy issues, is dominated by the search for the 'secret sauce' ... the insider who knows What's Really Going On. Background interviews with top officials are regarded as gold, and the desire to get those interviews often induces reporters to spin on demand.
>
> But such inside scoops are rarely — I won't say never, but rarely — worth a thing. My experience has been that careful analysis of publicly available information almost always trumps the insider approach. Reporters with top-level access got completely snookered by the lies about Iraq, while many ordinary concerned citizens, looking at what we actually seemed to know, figured out early on that the Bush administration was cooking up a false case for war.

Blogs had another advantage too, to which I've already alluded. Uninhibited by the need to cultivate sources or to stay in the good books of various politicians or other insiders, bloggers were able to offer an alternative reading of what the likes of George W. Bush, Dick Cheney, John Howard, and others were saying without having to worry about being 'cut off'. This is where standard journalistic practice actively mitigates against good journalism. The symbiotic relationship between the media and politicians leaves both sets of insiders vulnerable to each other's groupthink, even when one isn't consciously trying to cultivate the other.

As the Iraq War dragged on year after year, the blogosphere pored over the evidence and drew its own conclusions. We were no longer dependent on the mainstream media's interpretation of what was happening or who had said what, as indispensible as a lot of that reporting was. We had escaped the narrative, the official storyline that tends to emerge when a self-interested and self-replicating media reports from inside the church of the savvy. For the first time in history, a significant portion of the citizenry was able to play an active role in the large-scale creation and dissemination of information about a major news event. This was the new front page of journalism in the making. Undoubtedly it caused a rush of blood to the head in some of us, and there was a bit of blog triumphalism apparent, but the excitement we felt was justified. This was new. And it was important. This was democracy as if citizenship mattered, and no one should underestimate the sheer thrill of participation.

Many in the media, instead of learning from what we were doing, got their backs up, and so began the denigration of the blogosphere, or the users of social media more generally, which continues to this day. Some journalists have moved on from that initial hostility (if they ever exhibited it at all) and have started using the sorts of techniques we were using, but overall the industry remains captive to the old ways. This is especially noticeable in the way the mainstream continues to treat its audience. Some lip service is paid to the idea of interacting with readers and viewers, but the engagement is largely token and reactive.

If I had to cite the key difference between the way bloggers went about gathering and presenting information and the way mainstream journalists did it, I would say that we were readers and they were callers. This distinction might have its origins in the fact that a lot of the early bloggers, especially the ones who went on to dominate the form, were academics or had studied at university and were therefore trained to 'look things up' rather than go out and interview people. With more and more journalists now coming into the industry via university courses, this is obviously changing, but the culture of 'use the phone' still pervades the newsroom (not without reason). Journalists were and are trained on the job and are taught the importance of speaking to people directly, and of maintaining a list of contacts that they guard with their lives and cultivate and expand at every opportunity.

Journalists often criticise bloggers and other 'citizen journalists' for not using the phone more, and on one level, that's fair enough. But the fact is, journalists are licensed by democratic societies to confront people in a way that 'a person with a blog' is not, and so the criticism is not really fair. As I discovered, it is much easier to ring up the head of a company for comment when you are 'Tim Dunlop from News Limited' rather than 'Tim Dunlop, the guy with a blog'. So our modus operandi was as *readers*: we looked things up, and in the age of Google, the ease of access to, and sheer volume of, written material available online made it possible to draw upon vast reserves of information. We read our way into the topic and brought together all that we had read in a series of posts. If sometimes it was cursory and speculative in a way that was unacceptable to the professionals, that was okay, because as new information became available, or when a reader told us we had got something wrong, we could update the post or write a new one. We could respond in the comments box, and gradually work our way towards a better understanding. The very flexibility and tentativeness of the form were its greatest strengths because they went hand in hand with a transparency that was patently lacking in the way the mainstream media went about its job. We didn't bury our corrections weeks later on page 18; we integrated them into the posts themselves. We added updates and we linked to those who had a different point of view.

Finance journalist and blogger with Reuters Felix Salmon makes a similar point about the difference between bloggers and journalists. In one post he argues that the mainstream still hasn't learned to 'read' and that they are suffering because of it:

> [T]he biggest thing that's missing in the journalistic establishment is people who are good at finding all that great material, and collating it, curating it, adding value to it, linking to it, presenting it to their readers. It's a function which has historically been pushed into a blog ghetto, and which newspapers and old media generally have been pretty bad at. And of course old media doesn't understand blogs in the first place, let alone have the confidence or the ability to incorporate such thinking into everything they do.
>
> Think about it this way: reading is to writing as listening is to talking — and someone who talks without listening is both a boor and a bore. If you can't read, I don't want you in my newsroom. Because you aren't taking part in the conversation which is all around you.

Journalist Margaret Simons laments a similar lack in Australian journalists in her 2012 book, *Journalism at the Crossroads: crisis and opportunity for the press*. She notes how few journalists these days can do things such as company-title or land-title searches, and points out the failure of the Australian media to make important public-sector information widely available. She writes, 'I am sadder than I can reasonably express to say this, but in Australia all the important moves in this revolution are not being made by journalists, but by governments and engaged, web-savvy citizens, often on a volunteer and not-for-profit basis', and asks, 'Why didn't they [undertake such projects]? Could it be that they were instinctively preserving their privileged access to it? Whatever the motivation, the result is that professional journalists are becoming increasingly irrelevant to the act of searching for information.'

And in their extensive report into what they call 'post-industrial journalism', Clay Shirky and Emily Bell write:

> Too many reporters remain locked into a mindset where a relatively limited list of sources is still relied on to gather evidence for most important stories, with the occasional rewritten press release or direct observation thrown in. This insider-centric idea of original reporting excludes social media, the explosion of digital data, algorithmically generated sources of information, and many other new strategies of information gathering.

There was no brilliant insight that caused bloggers to go about our work in the way we did. We searched for, collated, curated, added value to, and linked alternative sources of information because these were the only tools available to us. In doing so, we stumbled across a way of communicating that is at least as valid as more traditional forms of reportage, and perhaps sometimes better. But it was how we presented the information that was the more important breakthrough: we talked to our readers and they talked to us. We stepped outside the top-down model of news dissemination and made it radically amateur. We put journalists under the same sort of sustained pressure to perform that they themselves like to use on the subjects of their enquiries, and that was no bad thing. We provided a way for ordinary people and various experts not just to voice their opinions or share their knowledge, but also to do so in a space in which they could interact as equals. We changed ourselves from passive consumers into active participants.

Still, the sheer amount of time conscientious blogging required made it impossible for many to keep up the pace. Some of my favourites, such as 'Jeanne' from the mighty *Body and Soul* blog, and Chris Sheil from *Back Pages*, simply closed up shop. One of my all-time favourites, Rob Corr, graduated from uni and got a job. Ken Parish at (as it is now called) *Club Troppo* invited others to join him and so developed the idea of a 'group blog'. Group blogs sprang up everywhere and some of them, like *Crooked Timber* in Britain and *Larvatus Prodeo* in Australia, were part of the next wave of superblogs that came to dominate the landscape.

We had also reached the outer limits of what it was possible to do as an amateur. It seemed to many of us that the only way to stay in the game was to figure out a way to make some money from what had become an obsessive hobby. Market forces intruded on something that we had viewed, up until then, as nothing more than civic engagement.

## CHAPTER THREE

# The Blogosphere Goes Professional

*Stop listening to newspaper people. We have had nearly*
*15 years to figure out the Web and as an industry we*
*newspaper people are no good at it. No good at it at all.*
*Want to get good at it? Then stop listening to the newspaper*
*people and start listening to the rest of the world.*
JOHN PATON, DIGITAL FIRST MEDIA CEO

By 2005 bloggers and blog readers were facing up to the
fact that, for all the optimism of the early days, our furious
public discussion and rumination hadn't made a blind bit of
difference.

Yes, we had exposed the structural and cultural
weaknesses of commercial media and the government
deception they had enabled, and yes, we were speaking
out about the shortcomings of longstanding journalistic
practices, but we were not being heard. The wars in Iraq
and Afghanistan continued; not one life was saved by a
blog post. George W. Bush was elected for a second term.
John Howard won another election, too, as did Tony Blair.
Our enthusiastic assault on mainstream misinformation
and deception was no triumph of participatory democracy

— not if the measure you use is the ability to translate such discussion into meaningful policy, into an ability to influence the way politics is conducted. Power remained pretty much where it was, untroubled by the glorious rise of blogging. As we hadn't so much forced our way into the national conversation as started our own, we remained easy to ignore, and the political class, including the media, took great delight in doing just that.

In crucial ways, we didn't change anything. But that doesn't mean nothing had happened.

Blogging was the beginning of the long arc of transformation brought about by the rise of new media, an arc whose end point is still unseeable around the never-ending bend of the future. Even though it would be more than a decade before the Australian mainstream media even *began* to take the new media seriously — when they discovered and fell in reluctant love with Twitter — even at this time, no one with half a brain was in any doubt that something fundamental had changed about the relationship between the media and its audience.

Few were better at capturing that changing mood than Duncan Black, the Philadelphia economist-turned-blogger who used the nom de plume of Atrios at his incredibly popular blog, *Eschaton*. He started talking about the 'very serious people' who ran the world. The phrase actually belongs to another blogger, Heather Parton, who uses the name Digby at her blog, *Hullabaloo*, and who to this day remains one of the most clear-headed commentators on the state of US politics. It was a term laced with sarcasm, but nobody in that thickening wood of blogs and comments threads had any trouble understanding every layer of its meaning. It was shorthand for those people in power who retained their power, no matter how badly they got things wrong; for those whose influence existed within a system designed to make them all but unsackable. Launch a failed war on the basis of doctored intelligence and wilful or accidental gullibility? No problem, your job will still be waiting for you tomorrow. Same when you cause the biggest financial meltdown since the Great Depression.

Black also popularised the term 'the village', his name for the professional media pack who reported politics in the mainstream, and who offered cover for 'the very serious people'. The name captured the profession in all its small-town self-obsession — its certainty in its own rightness about everything, no matter how often those certainties were contradicted by the facts. Black was talking about the American political reporting establishment, but there was an equivalent in Australia. The failures of reporting the Iraq War were just as apparent here, and went just as unpunished. Writing in *Bad News: Murdoch's Australian and the shaping of the nation*, Robert Manne said of Greg Sheridan, the head foreign policy writer for *The Australian*: 'The problem with Sheridan is not that he lacks eloquence or intelligence or even that he is so right-wing. The problem is that he lacks judgment and the capacity to learn from his many, many egregious mistakes,' and therefore, 'One of the greatest weaknesses of Chris Mitchell's editorship of *The Australian* is that he has allowed Greg Sheridan to remain his foreign editor throughout.'

There is a layer of insulation that slows down the transference of heated anger between those in and with power and those in the broader electorate. Slows down, but ultimately does not stop. At the end of his two terms George W. Bush's administration would be seen as a failure on multiple levels, and he would become a byword for political deception, to the extent that in the 2012 presidential campaign he was kept well away from the Republican Party National Convention that was reluctantly endorsing Mitt Romney. John Howard's government not only lost office in 2007, but he also became only the second prime minister in Australia's history to lose his own seat at a federal election. And Tony Blair was forced into early retirement, his sanctimonious justifications for the invasion of Iraq no longer believed and his credibility shot. (Of the three, it is John Howard's reputation that remains the least besmirched, which says something about the relative weakness of the Australian blogosphere and its power to shape debate in what is demonstrably the least diverse media market of any contemporary democracy.)

These changes mightn't have happened as quickly as some of us would've liked, but it is interesting to contemplate whether they would've happened at all without the sort of public discussion that blogs helped generate.

In 1997, Mark Davis wrote a book called *Gangland: cultural elites and the new generationalism*; in it he highlighted the way in which Australian political and cultural debate was dominated by a small, homogenous group of prominent public figures who ruthlessly guarded the gates of commentary in these areas. In 2007, writing in *The Age*, Davis revisited his thesis and found that pretty much the same people were still in charge:

> Many of the figures who stood out in 1997 as playing a disproportionate role in Australian cultural life by and large continue to do so. Kerry O'Brien, Robert Manne, Peter Craven, Phillip Adams, Christopher Pearson, Anne Summers, Helen Garner, Richard Neville, Keith Windschuttle, Ray Martin, Clive James, P.P. McGuinness, Germaine Greer, Piers Akerman, John Laws, Michelle Grattan, Laurie Oakes, Alan Jones, Gerard Henderson and George Negus are still out there, setting agendas, demarcating standards, creating much of the intellectual and cultural climate. Whatever they breathe out becomes the oxygen of Australian cultural life.
>
> Or, to shift metaphors, the gang is still in town.

More than half a decade further on, and many of those same names still dominate our media — an extraordinary fact when you consider not only the wholesale changes wrought upon the industry in the wake of its collapsing business model, but also that advances in technology have enabled so many new writers and thinkers to emerge. Literally thousands of journalists and ancillary staff have been sacked from newspapers and from television and radio stations, and yet this solid core of uber-commentators hangs on.

Why did the burgeoning blogosphere, and particularly political blogs, which had liberated so many interesting and informed writers, fail to penetrate the mainstream media? Let's look at the United States, where the gatekeepers responded in a way that their Australian counterparts did not.

As early as 2003, the mainstream political parties in the United States had been 'reaching out' (as they put it) to the blogosphere. Key bloggers were invited to conferences held by politicians, and politicians sought invitations to conferences held by bloggers. Yes, American bloggers became big enough and important enough to hold their own conferences. Markos Moulitsas, founder of *Daily Kos*, organised one of the major ones — called the YearlyKos, it was first held in Las Vegas in 2006, and has continued every year since (though now it is known as Netroots Nation and is part of a broader activist network associated with its parent company, Kos Media, LLC). Moulitsas himself, along with other bloggers, including Jerome Armstrong from the blog *MyDD*, was also hired by the 2004 Howard Dean presidential campaign to act as an adviser on 'internet outreach'. Beyond this sort of mixing between the mainstream political class and the blogosphere, politicians and their operatives made themselves available to bloggers for interviews, while parts of the traditional media began scouring the ranks of bloggers in order to recruit them.

Nothing remotely like any of this happened in Australia.

Political organising in Australia is immensely different from the United States, largely because we have compulsory voting and they do not. In its absence, the single biggest job parties and candidates in the United States face is 'getting out the vote', and it costs a fortune; enormous efforts need to be put into fundraising, and ensuring that issues are pitched in a way that overcomes voter inertia come election day. The main risk in US politics is not that your candidate will be outvoted, but that your potential voters will not turn up in sufficient numbers to get him or her over the line. When the first job you have to perform in politics is motivation, your appeals are going to be to those issues that you think will fire people up, so parties end up campaigning on divisive issues.

Bipartisanship can never be the motivator that tribal loyalty is, and simple works better than complicated. This has led to the dominance of topics that come from the so-called culture wars — matters of policy, sure, but matters that also reach deep into the flesh and blood and sinews of American values: gay marriage, abortion, guns, religion, and, of course, patriotism. In the early days of blogging, patriotism was arguably the single biggest motivator politicians employed to get out the vote, and the truth is, it was owned by the Republican Party. National security is a legitimate political issue, but the genius of right-wing campaigning was that it tied Republican views on the topic to the more general notion of love of country. To oppose the wars in Afghanistan and Iraq was to be unpatriotic; it was to be indifferent to the plight of the troops who were putting themselves in harm's way. It was to give comfort to the enemy. It was to be a Democrat.

It is not unreasonable to say that a good percentage of blogging, from the left, progressive side of the spectrum, was concerned with unpicking the phony logic of this sort of campaigning (while the right-wing blogs reinforced the message). The new form, with its unlimited space, was the perfect place to have that sort of discussion, and that's what we bloggers did — though many of us could just about have taken as our motto Churchill's comment that a lie can travel around the world before the truth has a chance to even put on its shoes and socks. Although such unpicking had no immediate impact on realpolitik, it did lay the groundwork for a left-of-centre resurgence as the mood of the country changed, the wars dragged on, and the spin of the war boosters could no longer outrun facts that by now were wearing their shoes and socks.

US political campaigning is also embedded in a money-driven framework that commits every politician to a career-long search for donors, and given that fact, it is little wonder that American politics is dominated by the concerns of those who finance it. Research by Martin Gilens, a political scientist at Princeton University, shows this to be the case. In his book *Affluence and Influence: economic inequality and political power in America*, he writes:

> Few people would expect [political] influence to be identical [among classes]: those with higher incomes and better connections will always be more influential. But if influence becomes so unequal that the wishes of most citizens are ignored most of the time, a country's claim to be a democracy is cast in doubt. And that is exactly what I found in my analyses of the link between public preferences and government policy in the U.S.

This turns on its head the usual presumption of democratic politics, which is that you have to broaden your electoral appeal so that you occupy the political centre in order to maximise your vote. The idea is that there are always enough swing voters (as they call them) to make it worthwhile pitching your campaign at them and that, almost by definition, such voters are repelled by policies that are considered partisan. However, George W. Bush, as he campaigned for a second term under the direction of Karl Rove, alighted on research that showed there are fewer swing voters than commonly believed. Thomas Edsall, writing at *The New Republic*, noted:

Between 1980 and 2000, the percentage of *true* swing voters fell from a very substantial 24 percent of the electorate to just 6 percent. In other words, the center was literally disappearing. Which meant that, instead of having every incentive to govern as 'a uniter, not a divider,' Bush now had every reason to govern via polarization.

Rove became wedded to the idea that you only needed 50.1 per cent of the vote in order to govern.

So blogs came into their own in the United States during a period of hyper-partisanship, and it is not surprising that they ended up reflecting that partisanship. Nor is it hard to see why US politicians would then be drawn to the blogosphere. Here was a group of ready-made communities, on the left or the right, with an engaged membership in sufficient numbers and with potentially sufficient clout to help parties with their get-out-the-vote and fundraising efforts. Years before the 2008 Obama campaign used social media to rake in millions of dollars in small donations, the 2002 mid-term elections and the 2004 presidential campaign saw many US blogs sporting donations buttons to allow their readers to donate to candidates and parties. *Eschaton* was so successful at this that it was written into a storyline for the television show *The West Wing*. The Josh Lyman character meets Atrios, the blog's owner, and tells a sceptical colleague that the blog raised 'three hundred grand' and that it has 'almost as many readers as *The Philadelphia Inquirer*'.

The point is, almost from the beginning, US blogs were tightly enmeshed with the mechanics of US politics in a way that was never echoed in Australia. This engagement (let's call it that rather co-option for the time being) between US politicians and the blogosphere lent US bloggers far more credibility than their Australian counterparts. Australian politicians, in part because of the existence of compulsory voting, had no need to even acknowledge the blogosphere and the public it was creating, and so they didn't. This was arguably short-sighted, but it was understandable, and it meant that no particular sense of influence or prestige ever attached to the communities that had formed within and around the blogosphere. Add in the fact that Australian political parties did not need to raise money in the same way US parties did — given that Australia not only has compulsory voting but also publicly financed elections — and there was even less reason for them to pay heed to blogs and their audience. The media happily followed the politicians' lead, though they had additional reasons for wishing to ignore what was happening online, as we've seen.

Compulsory voting in Australia helps to keep money out of politics and to ensure that a wider range of interests are taken seriously by politicians, but it also means that those regular citizens genuinely engaged in politics and public debate — those whom social media has christened 'wonks' and 'political tragics' — are seen by the political class to be unrepresentative of the broader public, to the point of being a nuisance. In America, such people have to be courted because they are the most likely, in the absence of government compulsion, to turn out to vote. In Australia, the same class of engaged citizens are held in contempt because they are making demands on the political class in the way that 'ordinary Australians' or 'normal people' aren't.

The bottom line is, the politicians and the mainstream Australian media pretty much chose to ignore the independent blogosphere as it developed. This is not to say that the media wasn't to be influenced by blogging's forms and style — they demonstrably would be — only that they would keep it in-house.

In the early days of blogging, I'm not sure that journalists really thought — as was sometimes asserted — that bloggers were a threat to their jobs, but they certainly sensed *some* sort of threat from the new technologies and those who wielded them. It must have been confronting to find your once-passive audience talking back, and that would certainly explain the contempt in which many journalists held the blogosphere. In this period of transition, those such as Hugh Martin, Margo Kingston, and Peter Martin, who embraced the possibilities of the online world and the new writers they uncovered, were the exception, not the rule.

It really isn't that surprising, of course. When you have spent an entire career building a reputation, cultivating sources, maybe sticking your neck out and taking personal risks to get stories, working long hours in a stressful undertaking, understanding yourself to be society's appointed guardian and part of a competitive profession in a market controlled by a small number of big players, you are unlikely to welcome a bunch of amateurs — literally amateurs, people who do at least some of what you do for money for free — into your ranks, no matter how good they are. And no matter how much they eschew the title of journalist and claim they are merely trying to participate in public debate as citizens.

Almost from the beginning, journalists used two tactics to counter any influence bloggers might have had. One was to belittle them personally, and so arose the oft-repeated depiction of bloggers as spoilt children. As Markos Moulitsas, founder of megablog *Daily Kos*, has said, 'Why, we were pajama-wearing buffoons living in our mother's basement, not very serious people like they were.' The other tactic was to assert their professional competence over the amateurism of blogging, something that has become a mainstay of journalistic pushback against blogs and other forms of social media. When Mark Scott, head of the Australian Broadcasting Corporation, commented in 2010 that journalists have to get used to the idea that media is now a 'shared space', then-senior News Limited journalist Caroline Overington responded:

Whatever Scott may think, journalism isn't easy. To illustrate the point: there was a time when reporters would send links to one another, perhaps with a short notes [*sic*], saying: 'Great piece.' You could open and read it, and chances are, it would be a great piece, meaning a beautifully written, thoughtful, sympathetic, clean piece of prose, written by somebody whose work had been beaten into shape by an army of editors and sub-editors over years.

See a link to a 'great piece' on Twitter nowadays, and you generally don't want to make the mistake of opening it, because chances are it will be absolute dross, produced by some clown with a cartoon character for a picture by-line, a fake name, no sense of perspective, and a good bit of bile in their gut.

'Great piece!' his mates will crow. 'You've nailed it!' But actually, it will be rubbish. In short, while most of us can boil an egg, *Masterchef* we ain't, and while most of us can apply a Band-Aid, we wouldn't attempt brain surgery. We can sing in front of the mirror, in other words, but let's not pretend to be Madonna.

Remember what I said about contempt?

Of course, reaction such as this from Overington misses the point. Whenever I read something like this I just want to tell the journalist, look, we know all that. We actually understand the importance of journalism; why else do you think we spend all this time reading it and writing about it? Sure, we criticise you, but we don't hate you. We just want you to do a better job — the same way you want politicians to do a better job when you point out their shortcomings.

I think it is fair to say that the overwhelming feeling within the blogosphere during this time was not one of contempt, and certainly not hate, but of disappointment.

But maybe that's the problem. Maybe journalists sensed the disappointment we bloggers felt, and that is what set them off. It is easier to deal with someone hating you than being disappointed in you. You can fight back against hatred, and be fairly certain the issue is your attacker. With disappointment, you are forced to confront something within yourself, and that is harder to do. Your enemies hate you; you can only disappoint your friends or admirers.

As sociologist Pierre Bourdieu said, journalists are part of 'a very powerful profession made up of very fragile individuals'. In this case, the problem was that they were expressing suspicion towards and questioning the credentials of their very own audience. Journalistic animosity thus . always risked becoming entirely self-defeating. Bloggers had created a place for themselves right on the thin line between the media as a market entity and the media as a civic entity, and on the equally thin line between journalist and citizen, and it made media professionals uncomfortable.

By refusing to seriously engage with the blogosphere, Australian journalists were acting as if they could maintain an arm's-length relationship with their audience. This was a failure of imagination, tied up with a jaunty bow of denial. They thus put off by around about a decade the mental adjustments needed to even begin to succeed in the new environment created by social media.

Much of the professionalisation of blogging that took place in the United States happened on the scale that it did because the market was big enough to support this transition. The first big breakthrough was the appearance of Blogads. Based in North Carolina, the company was launched in 2002 by the CEO of Pressflex LLC, Henry Copeland. Blogads was able to aggregate individual blogs into a single 'market' and thus interest advertisers in their combined reach. There were enough small and mid-size businesses to find this new (and cheap) market attractive, and so they started using it. I can remember seeing lots of ads for politically themed books spring up on blogs of both the left and the right, as well as ads for individual candidates. Suddenly, a number of part-time bloggers had an income. Blogads is entirely the reason why, for example, Duncan Black (Atrios of *Eschaton*) was able to quit his job as an economics professor and blog full-time. Markos Moulitsas is quoted on Blogads' Wikipedia page as saying, 'Blogads has been perhaps the single most important component to the rise of the liberal blogosphere.'

This influx of money had an immediate effect, and it changed the nature of blogging in the United States. It hardened the line between the 'big' bloggers, the ones with the most traffic, and those who were just along for the ride as engaged citizens. There were still plenty of people out there who had no particular desire to make blogging their livelihood, people who simply wanted to participate in the debate; but for many, that seemed like a lot less fun when their 'colleagues' were making a living out of it and were, as a consequence, being taken much more seriously.

Professionalisation also meant that it dawned on some mainstream journalists that if they had ever actually feared that bloggers were going to take their jobs, maybe that time had come — or was at least drawing closer. The competition might have been limited, but given the financial difficulties most of the media were having during this period (and of course continue to have), the presence of financed, organised blogging networks suddenly gave some substance to the fears.

A transition was well underway. Various bloggers got jobs with the 'legacy' media. The first amateur to move into the mainstream that I can remember was Matthew Yglesias, a young solo blogger, who was employed by *The American Prospect* magazine. He was duly christened 'Big Media Matt' by the blogosphere, and his 'promotion' was a genuine talking point for a good six months. Yglesias would, over the course of the next few years, move from *The American Prospect* to the Center for American Progress think tank, and then to *The Atlantic* magazine and, later, the online-only magazine *Slate*. The next move was made by Kevin Drum, who went to the *Washington Monthly* and, a few years later, to *Mother Jones*. *American Prospect* also picked up Ezra Klein, who is now a key journalist for *The*

*Washington Post*. And Duncan Black is a senior fellow at the Media Matters for America think tank, although he stills runs *Eschaton*.

There were other bloggers, generally ones who were journalists before they gained success in the blogosphere, such as Josh Marshall, who continued to make a living by freelancing in conjunction with their blogging. Far from typical, but certainly noteworthy, was Andrew Sullivan, the US-based British journalist who had, among other things, been the editor of *The New Republic*, but who came into his own when he launched his solo blog. It became so popular that when he decided to throw himself a fundraiser and ask his readers to donate to the work he was essentially doing for free, he raised in the vicinity of £80,000. Later, he went to *The Atlantic* and was part that magazine's revival, which was built around its stable of bloggers; he then went to *The Daily Beast*, a new-media start-up; and has most recently gone out on his own again, canvassing contributions from his readers — in the first six months of operation, he raised $715,000.

During the same period, established journalists such as Eric Alterman, James Fallows, Greg Mitchell, Charles Pierce, and many others started using blogs as the primary outlet for their work. Again, this was largely sustained by the mid-size magazines and think tanks, and only later spread to the larger mainstream outlets such as *The Washington Post* and *The New York Times*.

Soon enough, blogs such as *Talking Points Memo* and *The*

*Huffington Post* became fully fledged media organisations, and they started to employ professional journalists in their own right. Magazines as disparate as *Esquire* and *The Nation* hosted political bloggers, or rebadged their columnists as bloggers.

In short, what was happening was less a professionalisation of the blogosphere than a complete change in what we meant by the idea of the media. This was convergence, a part of the massive realignment of resources unleashed by the digitisation of news. It served to underline just how problematic it was to think of what was happening as an us-against-them phenomenon. The mainstream media, to this day, still likes to present the argument as one of journalists versus bloggers or other users of social media, but the truth is, from the very beginning of this transformation the lines have been hopelessly blurred. Journalists have blogged and bloggers have practised journalism.

Some of this was also happening in Australia, though in different ways. There is a temptation to presume that the sheer scale of what was happening in the United States meant that they were somehow doing new media better than we were, that their audiences and industry were more switched on to the new forms than ours, and that therefore what happened there is somehow not only a more developed form of what we have but also the inevitable shape of what we are heading towards. That is not necessarily so. The way the blogosphere developed in

America is not better or worse than the way it developed in Australia; nor are we inevitably heading down the same path. Each nation came with its own traditions and practices in which its old and new media environments were embedded, and thus the two were always likely to develop differently.

Still, if the issue is commercialisation, then the smaller market in Australia meant that not only was it harder for an organisation such as Blogads to arise, but also that we lacked almost entirely the range of mid-size magazines and think tanks that facilitated the professionalisation of the blogosphere in the United States. Certainly, my blog, *The Road to Surfdom*, was only able to attract advertising while I was based in the States — not enough to live on by any means, but more than enough to cover hosting costs and other expenses associated with the site and then some; but most of that dried up once I was back in Australia. I made a number of attempts to interest relevant Australian businesses in advertising on *Surfdom* — for instance, several book publishers — but there was no interest, just bemusement. At different times between 2004 and 2006 I was approached by other Australian bloggers who were attempting to launch some sort of group site with an eye to selling advertising space, and although a number of these attempts were well-thought-out, serious ventures with legitimate business plans, they failed to attract any funding. *Crikey* and *On Line Opinion* were more successful, but they were pretty much exceptions to the rule.

I can't help but feel that the bigger issue was a lack of imagination among the Australian business community. I'd experienced it before — back in the early 1980s, when I'd opened that video library, one of Melbourne's first. This was well before the days of the easy credit that kicked in from about the late 1990s, and it was impossible, literally impossible, to interest any bank in helping to finance anything as new-fangled as a video library. The same problem confronted us with insurance, and in dealings with the local council: in those days, insurance premiums on videos in a retail outlet were so high that there was no way we could afford them, so we used to carry our entire stock home every night so it was covered by our home insurance; we were also approached by the local council not long after we opened and told that as they had no particular zoning requirements for a video library, they had decided to treat us as a restaurant, and so we would have to install a public toilet and provide x number of car spaces. I forget how we talked them out of that.

I could see the same fear of the new in how Australian businesses — and politicians and the media — responded to blogs and other online sites. There was a wait-and-see approach to the whole thing, and maybe this is partly a difference in attitude between the United States and Australia, or maybe it is simply another side effect of the difference in market size. Regardless, there was a sense in which the blogosphere was becoming more professionalised, and it had its own momentum. Many of those involved in blogging enjoyed it, were good at it, and were becoming keen to derive some income from it.

I was certainly one of those looking for opportunities to make some money from blogging. As it happened, it wasn't long after I returned to Australia that I got an offer to join the mainstream media.

## CHAPTER FOUR

# *Diving into the Mainstream*

*I'm a writer by profession and it's totally clear to me that
since I started blogging, the amount I write has increased
exponentially, my daily interactions with the views of others
have never been so frequent, the diversity of voices I engage with
is far higher than in the pre-Internet age — and all this has
helped me become more modest as a thinker, more open to error,
less fixated on what I do know, and more respectful of what I don't.
If this is a deterioration in my brain, then more, please.*

ANDREW SULLIVAN, AUTHOR AND BLOGGER

The idea that I would, after more than four years writing
a left-of-centre political blog as an independent citizen
beholden to no one except my readers and myself, start
writing a blog for the most buttoned-down, conservative
news organisation in the country, a mob I'd spent a fair bit
of time criticising and thumping the desk over, was not
something I would've bet a lot of money on. If I was going
to get an offer from anyone — and the possibility never
remotely occurred to me — I would've guessed I would be
of more interest to Fairfax than to News Limited. Not that
I thought Fairfax was particularly left-wing (don't make me

laugh), just that I knew News Limited was unashamedly right of centre, and I figured that if I was on their radar at all, it probably had more to do with aiming darts than making job offers.

But there it was one day towards the end of 2005, out of the blue: an email asking me if I'd like to write a blog for the biggest media organisation in the country. Nothing much went through my head except for *yes*. I knew I'd get grief from some people once it became public, and I knew there were other risks involved, but to me it was perfectly logical. The whole point of blogging, of having discussions about important issues online, was to engage in argument in public, and not just with people who agreed with you, but with people who didn't. In that sense, I would actually prefer to work for an openly right-of-centre organisation. I wouldn't go so far as to say I wanted to change people's minds about anything, not in any sort of proselytising sense, but I was pretty committed to the idea that public debate was an end in itself and that democracy needed a healthy culture of talking about politics from all perspectives. If going to News Limited opened up a potentially bigger and more diverse audience, great. If they would pay me to do it, even greater.

The offer had been a long time in the making. Before I left the United States, Hugh Martin from Fairfax had contacted me. Hugh was editor of theage.com.au, and part of their online development team. He also ran a media blog on the *Age* site. We'd previously chatted via email and the comments threads at *Surfdom*, so I knew who he was. He said he was going on leave and asked if I would like to fill in for him on the *Age* blog. There was no pay involved, but I thought, what the hell.

Like a lot of bloggers back then, I was still a bit in thrall to the convenient fiction that exposure is as good as a pay cheque: information wants to be free and all that nonsense. I remember hearing Phillip Adams chatting to Margo Kingston, when she did her regular spot on his radio show, about *Webdiary* and the way her readers (the likes of me) sent her content for free. Adams was appalled that people would write for no pay, and at the time I thought, yeah, but we're not in it for the money. And we weren't. But after a couple of years of blogging more or less for free, the novelty had worn off.

I had seen a lot of US bloggers suddenly start to earn money for what they were doing, and I could see no reason why Australia's bloggers shouldn't avail themselves of some income if someone was offering. It went through my head that if I could make a good fist of it with one of the major media groups, it would become that much more likely that other bloggers would be offered paying gigs, too. I knew blogging had unearthed writers who had the talent and skills to reinvigorate our public debate, and I genuinely thought that it was only a matter of time before they started making their way into paid work in the mainstream.

So I knew Hugh Martin from his Fairfax days, but in early 2005 he had moved to News Limited to head up their online operations, and it was he who contacted me to ask if I was interested in writing a blog for his new employer. Hugh worked for a News Limited subsidiary called News Interactive, and it was that entity to which I would eventually be contracted. The significance of this wasn't apparent to me when I first signed on, but in some ways it is vital to understanding how things unfolded over the next few years.

News Interactive ran News Limited's online operations. This included all the websites for the company's main mastheads — everything from *The Mercury* in Hobart to their national broadsheet, *The Australian* — as well as their central and increasingly popular general news site, news.com.au. News Interactive was a small operation in the greater scheme of News Limited, and only employed a few of its own journalists. Most of the material on news.com.au came from the mastheads themselves, and this made News Interactive rather a supplicant organisation: it relied almost entirely on the goodwill of the masthead editors for the bulk of its content, and once I started it became apparent to me very quickly that this meant News Interactive was, to a certain extent, in a constant state of low-level war with the mastheads.

But to go back a step: in November 2005 I met Hugh at an Adelaide cafe and we talked about the sort of thing I would do for them. It was all pretty straightforward: they wanted me to keep doing what I had been doing at *Surfdom*. In fact, one suggestion he made was that I simply move *The Road to Surfdom* to the news.com.au site and continue there, but I wasn't really tempted; I wanted to keep *Surfdom* separate. John Quiggin had managed something similar with his personal site and his work at the group blog *Crooked Timber*, so I knew it was possible. No conditions were mentioned, though it was clear that on their part the whole project was pretty experimental; and, it is important to note, it was a commercial experiment: News Interactive was interested in building up a stable of bloggers covering a range of topics, and I would do politics.

After an amiable and uncontroversial chat, Hugh said, 'You do realise that News Limited is a pretty conservative organisation, don't you?'

'I wondered when that was going to come up,' I said, admiring his facility for understatement.

'Will it be a problem?' he asked.

I said something along the lines of, 'Well, I presume I should limit my attacks on Rupert Murdoch to about one a week?'

This was pretty much the extent of our conversation on the subject, but the point he was trying to make, I think, was that there would be limits on what I could write. He wasn't telling me that I had to watch myself, or that people would need to approve what I wrote, or any of the usual stuff people think of when they imagine the media controlling writers; it was just that I was no longer going to be in the blogosphere where I was entirely my own boss and where even the laws of slander and defamation were only weakly enforced. The exact boundaries between what I could and couldn't do were impossible to define in advance, but he was telling me that they existed.

What I understood from this brief conversation was that I would be in an environment that would be hostile to a lot of the pieces I wrote and that although no one was likely to interfere directly, I would probably feel the pressure.

The interference, when it came — and it did come — was completely unexpected and entirely predictable.

Between our chat in the Adelaide cafe and the launch of the site there were many, many emails. We tossed around ideas for a name and eventually settled on *Blogocracy*. The word had some currency in the blogosphere, but much to my surprise, a series of searches revealed that no one had ever used it as the name for a blog. Combining the word 'blog' with 'democracy' captured exactly the vibe (yes, I said vibe) I was going for with the new site, and so we locked it in.

We also talked about the way comments would be handled. On *Surfdom*, and on most blogs at that time, there was no initial moderation of comments: if someone left a comment, it would appear immediately on the site. If something was published that you, as the site owner, deemed unacceptable, you could always delete it. If the same commenter kept posting rubbish, creating a problem, you could keep deleting. In fact, some of the newer blog software, such as WordPress, had a facility where you could either put an individual commenter into moderation or block them altogether; though in those days, blocking and putting people into moderation were not the done thing.

But News Limited was not the blogosphere. Like most mainstream-media organisations, they insisted that comments go through a moderating process. That is, the comment would be held in a queue, unpublished, until someone read it, approved it, and let it appear on the site. This was designed to protect the company against the risk of publishing something that was likely to get them sued. I was reluctant for *Blogocracy* to use a moderation queue, as it meant the whole process of interaction with the audience was slowed down considerably, so I tried to make a case for unmoderated comments. But it was an argument I was always going to lose. There was no way on Rupert's green earth that they were going to allow comments to be published unmoderated. This was a nuisance, and flew in the face of the sort of fast-paced exchanges that I considered to be the heart and soul of blogging.

News Limited's concerns about legal action were reasonable — rational, even — but I doubt rationality was the only reason for demanding comment moderation. The entire model of mainstream journalism is predicated on top-down control; as Rupert Murdoch himself has said, he 'grew up in a highly centralized world where news and information were tightly controlled by a few editors, who deemed to tell us what we could and should know'. Producing a newspaper, a television program, or a radio show is an exercise in having the power to decide what gets published and what doesn't. Control flows from proprietors to editors and down through the chain of management to the various levels of journalists. The idea of comment moderation fits very snugly into a model that at every point seeks to control what constitutes 'the news'. Allowing readers' comments to make it onto a website without some sort of oversight, some sort of editorial control, was anathema to an industry so used to gatekeeping; it was simply not regarded as a possibility. I don't doubt that there were genuine concerns about legal action arising from unmoderated comments, but it would be naïve to think that that was all there was to it.

*Blogocracy* was finally launched on 6 November 2006, and so began a two-year experiment in which new media met old. I was the first Australian blogger to be employed by the mainstream media — we were breaking new ground, learning as we went. The reaction from my readers at *Surfdom* and among the wider blogosphere was overwhelmingly positive, though there were dissenters who saw me as some sort of sell-out. Of course, I disagreed with that assessment, but it doesn't mean that such concerns weren't legitimate. Perhaps if my critics had known just how badly I was being paid they would've at least rethought the use of the term 'sell-out'.

On the whole, I ignored the criticism. I figured the best way of addressing it was to get on with the job of blogging, and that's what I did.

In my first post I outlined what I was trying to do:

[T]he idea here is to pick apart the issues of the day in the way that normal human beings talk about such things. This is less about journalism than it is about citizenship, the idea that all of us have a say in how the country is run and that participation is a good thing in its own right ...

Like you, I'm totally reliant on the ability of journalists everywhere to go out and get the stories on which our discussion here will depend. If you think of those guys as the first responders who show up when something important happens, then this blog is kind of like the forensic team that shows up later and picks over what others have already found.

I'm also sure you'll quickly detect any biases I have on given topics, but don't let it worry you: I'm not exactly going to hide them. That said, I've got no interest in ignoring facts and I'm open to be swayed by evidence (it's not a rightwing blog, after all). Use the comments section to show me where I'm wrong. In fact, use the comments section to discuss things with other readers, to make suggestions, to pass on relevant links, or tip me off about something you think I should blog about. I don't promise to follow up on every suggestion, but I'll do my best to respond asap ... [C]heck in regularly. There'll be a lot going on.

Things started fairly slowly — that first post only received 14 comments — but *Blogocracy* soon built a dedicated following, and the comments box filled up with a band of regulars.

It turned out that Hugh Martin left News Limited not long after I started and so my immediate boss became the newly appointed editor of news.com.au, David Higgins. He and his deputy, Paul Colgan, were my main points of contact with the organisation. I was also in regular contact with the tech people, and maybe this was the biggest difference between the amateur blogosphere and the mainstream media, having access to what seemed like a whole department of experts to deal with technical issues. What a joy that was! No more playing around on Google trying to teach myself code or relying on the goodwill of generous readers who had the relevant skills. Guys such as Rod Peno and Lincoln Archer were not only tech experts, but also totally committed to building online journalism. They sent around links to articles discussing various aspects of the business and were keen to hear what someone like me, with experience out there in the wilds of the blogosphere, thought about key issues. My brain was picked regularly, and I was always glad to be involved in the discussion.

The truth is, everyone at News Interactive made me feel very welcome. I was given all the help I needed, and *Blogocracy* was happily promoted on the front page of the news.com.au website, even when I was criticising other parts of the company. I think I got a much better run from News Limited than professional journalist Margo Kingston got from Fairfax in her *Webdiary* days.

There was almost no difference between *Blogocracy* and *Surfdom* in terms of the sorts of topics I covered and the way I covered them. Occasionally a blogger somewhere would make some snide remark about me now being under the control of the Murdoch Borg, but if anything, I was amazed at how hands-off my editors were. I certainly sometimes got requests from them to cover a particular issue, but the requests were always very specifically about the topic, not the approach I took to it, and it was always a request. Sometimes I'd just say no, it wasn't my sort of thing, and I was never made to feel that that was a problem. Sometimes I'd have a crack at it and then abandon the post because I didn't think I was adding anything valuable. Most often, the requests came through and I was writing about it anyway because it involved some relevant, breaking political news story. When that happened, the only difference between how I responded at *Blogocracy* and how I would've responded at *Surfdom* was the timeframe: I could take my own sweet time at *Surfdom* (though you still wanted to respond as quickly as possible), whereas at *Blogocracy* there was often an actual deadline.

I did try to align what I was writing much more closely with the day's news cycle than I had at *Surfdom*. That is to say, I was more inclined to bounce off the lead story of the day for my opening post each morning, in order to allow the editorial staff to link to it elsewhere on the news.com. au site. To be on top of the day's news, I started work at

5.00 a.m. and scoured the local and international news, trying to get my head around what the editors of the world had decided was important on that day so that I could say something useful about it.

I averaged about four posts daily. This wasn't an earth-shattering number by blogging standards, but it was pretty decent, especially given most of them were reasonably substantial pieces, not just quick posts with links to other sites. And this doesn't include the interaction I had with readers in the comments box. Talking to people, responding to their comments and their criticisms, added thousands more words to my daily tally.

By the time I finished moderating comments and switched off for the day, it was at least 11.00 p.m.

But it was a hoot and I loved almost every minute of it. Traffic to the site was on an upward trajectory, according to the figures I was shown, and the weekly emails we got listing the most commented-upon and most trafficked-to sites across the News Limited network often showed *Blogocracy* posts in the top ten in both categories. The comparison was not only with the few other blogs that News Limited ran, but with every article and column published online across their mastheads — from, say, Andrew Bolt's blog to a column by Paul Kelly. *Blogocracy* more than held its own, to the extent that I was getting emails from others at News Limited asking me to link to pieces they had written in order to drive traffic to their sites. Such requests always came from people such as Joe Hildebrand or Evan Maloney, writers who were most at home in the new-media environment and understood the value of that sort of networking. It made me aware of the divide within the organisation between those who embraced online and those who didn't.

In my ongoing dealings with the editors at News Interactive, the division between new and old media was a constant topic of conversation. It's fair to say that there was a degree of hostility between the online operations and those of the traditional newspapers; not among everyone in these two divisions, of course, but I certainly got the impression that News Interactive saw themselves as a progressive vanguard among a significant number of journalists and editors whom they thought just didn't 'get it'. It was blindingly obvious that as a blogger at News Interactive I was in the middle of a battle between old and new ways. I don't mean to imply that I was central to such battles; far from it. I was totally peripheral in terms of actual influence. I just mean that the way I did my work was constantly affected by this internecine struggle.

The first time I ever got any concrete sense that *Blogocracy* was ruffling feathers within the organisation was when I wrote a post criticising a column by Janet Albrechtsen. The reaction also showed me that News Limited was not quite the ideological monolith it was often portrayed as.

The Albrechtsen post was one of those crazy right-wing rants about freedom that actually seemed to me to be more about curtailing freedom than enhancing it. Her argument was that we couldn't afford to extend the protections of our laws to anyone accused of terrorism; that we had to destroy the village in order to save it. I wrote a post saying this was risible, and concluded, 'It's easy to be a freedom-respecting liberal when there is no threat. Quite a bit harder when there is.'

The piece appeared on *Blogocracy*, but it was also featured on the front page of news.com.au. That is, my editors at News Interactive had given it a prominent spot on News Limited's flagship website — hardly the action of people trying to stifle dissenting opinion or push a company line. Still, I was informed later in the week that they had had some internal complaints about the piece, though I wasn't told who the criticism had come from. I was expecting to be instructed to back off or something similar, but was instead told that they were quite pleased with the ructions. 'At least it means they're paying attention,' the deputy editor told me, and that was that.

Occasionally I also locked horns with my editors. I wrote a piece that was critical of what I considered some boilerplate union-bashing by journalist Sid Marris, and I got into rather a heated (though non-hostile) discussion about it with Paul Colgan. He was concerned that I didn't understand how an article was put together and had thus directed my ire at the wrong person. My complaint was that the opening paragraphs of the story sought to cast a matter of union business in the worst possible light and that you had to read well into the piece to find that those accusations were contradicted by the facts; in other words, the story was structured with a sensationalist, anti-union lead, and the relevant details were buried deep in the article. Paul's point was that this wasn't necessarily Sid Marris's fault but reflected a decision made by a subeditor. I hadn't fully realised the extent to which a journalist's work could be reshaped by a subeditor, so perhaps I was blaming the wrong person. Still, I told him, it was knee-jerk union bashing, whoever was responsible, and that was the point of my post. And that's where the discussion ended. There was never the slightest suggestion that I should remove or alter the piece.

The incident highlighted what an experiment a site such as *Blogocracy* was for a mainstream-media organisation. It wasn't just that I took a more left-of-centre stance than the organisation as a whole, but also that I was more or less unencumbered by the usual editorial controls that are standard operating procedure for journalists. Like Margo Kingston at *Webdiary*, I had discovered that online writing was accorded a freedom not commonly available to print journalists, a freedom that arose from genuine experimentation. There was a sense that the organisation itself didn't really know what it was doing with something like *Blogocracy*, as well as a clear feeling that the online operation was of secondary importance to the 'real' work done by the mastheads, the daily newspapers printed with ink and sold in shops. I'm positive that my post would never have made it past an editor and into a newspaper in the pre-internet days; the very idea of someone within the organisation regularly writing articles that were critical of the methods and processes of that organisation was itself a new thing.

The primacy of the mastheads and their editors slowly started to filter through to me. The mastheads were where the power was. The matter even arose in a conversation I had with Andrew Bolt, the *Herald Sun*'s right-wing columnist and blogger. He had written a piece criticising me for a post that appeared on *The Road to Surfdom*. I was still occasionally cross-posting between *Surfdom* and *Blogocracy*, but I had asked a couple of my old commenters to take over the site and they were now keeping it running. They were doing a great job, but one of them wrote an ill-considered piece that made a joke about assassinating John Howard. When I saw it, I removed the post, and the person who wrote it was extremely apologetic and knew it had been an error of judgement. Nonetheless, Andrew Bolt had decided it was a good stick to beat me with, and had written a post doing just that.

I mentioned it in passing to Paul Colgan, and he suggested I ring Bolt and talk about it. I did, and Andrew and I had a pleasant chat. He promised to update his post — which he later did, noting that I had removed the offending piece — and our conversation turned to *Blogocracy* more generally. He wanted to know how I was finding it, and was generous in his comments about what I was doing. But, he said, if I really wanted to make a name for myself (did I?), I had to get off that silly News Interactive site and get myself a spot at one of the mastheads. That's where the action was, he assured me, and the sooner I signed up with one of them, the better off I would be. He went so far as to say that News Limited, and specifically the paper he worked for, the *Herald Sun*, needed a credible voice from the left, and that he would speak to his editor. (Nothing ever came of it.)

Meanwhile, News Interactive was under pretty constant pressure from the mastheads because of news.com.au. I was told that the masthead editors were getting more and more miffed about the website sourcing just about all its content from them. The argument was that news.com. au was stealing traffic from their sites — something, in my naivety, I had trouble getting my head around. Could one part of the same organisation really be that possessive and competitive? I was also surprised that the mastheads apparently didn't understand the networking effects of the online environment. With a bit of care, they could make news.com.au work for them, using it to drive traffic their way. Under David Higgins' leadership, it was becoming one of the most trafficked-to sites in Australia; surely that was a good thing for the mastheads and for the company more generally?

It wasn't necessarily seen that way, I learned. In fact, as Paul Colgan told me after another piece I'd written had met with disapproval somewhere in the organisation, the mastheads often threatened News Interactive with being cut off from their content. He said he feared that one day he was going to come to work and be told that they could no longer source content from such-and-such a masthead. To me (him too) it seemed a crazy way to operate, but I had no reason to doubt what I was being told.

Eventually the moment came when all the invisible lines of demarcation that I had been happily ignoring — had perhaps even convinced myself didn't exist, given the genuine and ongoing support I received from my editors — became visible. I finally put my foot on the third rail of News Limited's lines of power, and its name was Chris Mitchell.

Mitchell was the editor of *The Australian*, a paper at that time known in the blogosphere as the Government Gazette because of the less-than-adversarial approach it took to reporting the Howard government. As unprofitable as the paper was, it wielded quite a bit of influence in Australian political circles, and it didn't hesitate to use that influence to pursue a particular political agenda. It wasn't entirely uncritical of the Howard government, but not even its most avid supporters would have pretended it was anything other than a right-of-centre shill. (Okay, they mightn't have said shill, but the point stands.)

The problem that arose was not ideological — not entirely, anyway. I had written a post defending Peter Brent, the psephological blogger then writing at his own site, *Mumble*. 'Who says the mainstream media don't pay attention to the blogosphere?' the post began, and continued:

Yesterday, Peter Brent noted that he had fallen foul of some of those at *The Australian*:

*A courtesy call from Editor-in-Chief Chris Mitchell this morning informed me that the paper is going to 'go' Charles Richardson (from Crikey) and me tomorrow. Chris said by all means criticise the paper, but my 'personal' attacks on Dennis [Shanahan, political journalist at The Australian] had gone too far, and the paper will now go me 'personally'.*

*No, I'm not making this up.*

*If they only get as personal as I get with Dennis, then it should be tame, as I don't believe I've ever criticised anything other than his writing. And to think I described Dennis, in a chapter in a book being launched this month, as (with no sarcasm) 'a fine journalist'.*

*All very strange. And — I'd be lying if I didn't admit — a little stomach-churning.*

The editorial is up this morning and yes, they do 'go' Peter Brent ...

There are a number of things to say about all of this. The first is that the editorial is as much concerned about charges of bias against *The Australian* as anything else. This is how it begins:

*The measure of good journalism is objectivity and a fearless regard for truth. Bias, nonetheless, is in the eye of the beholder and some people will always see conspiracy when the facts*

*don't suit their view of the world. This is the affliction that*
*has gripped, to a large measure, Australia's online news*
*commentariat that has found passing endless comment on*
*other people's work preferable to breaking real stories and*
*adding to society's pool of knowledge.*

If bias is in the eye of the beholder, then there are a lot of 'beholders' out there who think *The Australian* is biased, particularly in its coverage of polling data. The evidence for this is not just to [be] found in the blogosphere but on their own pages where their columns and articles often fill up with criticism from their own readers accusing them of spinning information in favour of the Howard Government. In attacking the 'online commentariat' they are also attacking a sizeable sampling of their own readership …

What's interesting is that *The Australian* seems to believe that only they are capable of objectivity and they reject entirely any charge of bias. This is odd given that Chris Mitchell himself has said:

*Can I say something about* The Australian's *contribution to*
*the national political debate. It has made, as a newspaper, a*
*remarkable contribution, I think back over the last 10 years*
*that this government has been in office and I think of the*
*positions taken by* The Australian *newspaper.*

*It has been broadly supportive, generously so, of the*
*government's economic reform agenda. And it has been*
*a strong supporter, consistently … of industrial relations*

*reform. Its only criticism of the government is that it might*
*not have gone far enough ...*

*I think editorially and on the Op Ed page, we are right-*
*of-centre. I don't think it's particularly far right, I think some*
*people say that, but I think on a world kind of view you'd say*
*we're probably pretty much where* The Wall Street Journal,
*or* The Telegraph *in London are. So, you know, centre-right.*

... So I think the editorial is ill-conceived and way off
the mark in singling out Peter Brent in the way that it does.
His site largely confines itself to interpretation and in doing
so, provides a great service. The idea that he can't comment
without the editor of *The Australian* ringing him up to say
they are going to 'go' him is disturbing ... *The Australian* is,
of course, completely free to defend themselves, but it might
also pay them to reflect on why so many people see them as
the 'government gazette' rather than just dismiss nearly all
such criticism as 'a waste of time'.

The post is a robust but measured criticism of what
I considered an abuse of journalistic power. Given that
so much of what I wrote was about the way in which the
media covered politics, as well as the relationship between
new media and old, I simply wouldn't have been doing
my job if I had ignored Brent's story. Of course, there are
a million different ways I could've pitched it, but I chose
the method I always used, a consideration of the facts and
a firm expression of my conclusions. In the usual manner of

the blogosphere, everything was linked so that people could read, in their entirety and in context, the other pieces I was referring to, and I was happy to respond via future posts or in comments to any criticisms that might arise. Business as usual, in other words.

Except it wasn't. The post was removed by News Interactive editor David Higgins, after he — through other staff, I believe — was informed of a rather bracing call from Chris Mitchell. Higgins hadn't been in the office at the time but was told that Mitchell had expressed his displeasure in no uncertain terms. Such were their relative levels of power within the organisation that Higgins didn't really have much choice but to delete my post. He later told me that he regretted taking it down, that had he been in the office at the time things might've been different; but now that it was down, there was no way he could repost it.

I was working from home on another post while this was unfolding. The first I heard about the piece being removed was when I got an email from a reader. I was surprised, and at first not entirely sure what had happened. More emails began to land in my inbox. Not long afterwards, Paul Colgan contacted me; he told me the post had been taken down and that David Higgins would ring me once he got back to the office. Colgan didn't offer much detail, but he made it clear that Chris Mitchell was … unhappy.

The whole event caused a fairly major and instantaneous ripple through the political blogosphere, and those corners of the rest of the media that paid attention to such things. A number of journalists asked me for comment, but as I didn't really know what was happening, I declined. I was getting quite a few emails from readers by this point, and so published a brief post saying I would explain later in the day. It didn't turn out to be that easy. By now, several blogs and their comments threads were discussing the matter. A few had even rescued the deleted post from Google's cache and reposted it on their own sites. For the most part the discussion was sensible. The exception was among those half-a-dozen people who were still upset I'd gone to News Limited in the first place; a deleted post, of course, just proved that they'd been right all along. As self-serving as such criticism tended to be, it wasn't without some merit. I'd had a perfectly legitimate post removed because it had upset someone with the power to make it go away. In terms of independent journalism, it was a serious issue, and I was now very keen to talk with my editor.

My conversation with David Higgins extended over the next few days, via email and phone. I expressed my displeasure, and he was genuinely apologetic about the way it had been handled. He was also very firm about what he saw as the need to remove the post. He cited relationships with the mastheads in general and *The Australian* in particular, but he also said that he thought it wasn't the sort of content we should be running. He told me that in his opinion, internecine fighting of this sort was boring for readers, and that our job was to address matters of broader public interest. Initially my intention was to have the post restored, but it didn't take long for me to realise that that would never happen.

The discussion then became about how to respond. I wanted to explain to my readers what had happened. I also wanted to respond to rumours that I had quit, or was on the verge of doing so: I had told David that I thought I should quit, but he had talked me out of it, and he was very adamant about it. I was a bit surprised by this, but it showed that things had not degenerated to the extent I thought they had, and that my fears that I would now somehow be placed on a short leash were probably unfounded. So I told David that I thought we needed to explain to people what had happened, and suggested the following post:

> Last week a post of mine was pulled from this site and in the wake of that I quit. Two things have happened that have made me reconsider. First, the people here at News Interactive were keen for me to stay. They didn't want *Blogocracy* to close down. I was also swamped with emails from readers who had heard rumours of me quitting and were asking me not to. I have been completely overwhelmed by the support I have received. I mean that: overwhelmed. Thank you to all those who have written to say how much they value the site.
>
> On that basis alone, I've decided to stay. I'm not sure if I'm doing the right thing, but I figure it's worth a try, if only to repay the support *Blogocracy* has received. So let's see how it goes. Thanks again to everyone.

David considered it overnight, but the next day told me he didn't think it was a good approach to take. His logic was that any sort of acknowledgement of what had happened would just keep the issue alive, and the sooner we moved on, the better. I was keen to move on, too, but I wanted to explain to my readers. David said he understood, but that that wasn't how it worked. You think of these people as your peers, he told me, but you're playing with the big boys now and you don't need to explain. You just write the next post and keep going.

Such a view was hardly unusual in the mainstream media, but it was an almost perfect illustration of the culture clash between the values of the independent blogosphere and those of the for-profit commercial mainstream media; between the bottom-up attitude of blogging, where as a writer your relationship was first and foremost with your readers, and the top-down reality of the mainstream, where everything was determined by hierarchy, and where the readers — at least insofar as having anything to do with the internal machinations of the organisation — were a complete irrelevance. Each approach made perfect sense on its own terms, and I don't mean to criticise David Higgins. My post had put him in difficult position, and although I didn't think it should've been removed, I appreciated his willingness to talk the issues through.

Higgins, at least, understood that there were issues to be debated, but not everyone who commented on the matter did. Journalist Tim Blair, who by now was running a blog for *The Daily Telegraph*, saw it entirely from the viewpoint of someone safely ensconced within the power structures of the organisation. He wrote: 'This morning a Dunlop piece, again critical of *The Australian*, was pulled. No big deal. It was always going to happen. If you're going to consistently attack a particular enterprise, it's probably best not to be employed by that same enterprise. Lefties struggle with this simple concept.'

This reveals an amazingly narrow idea of public discussion, let alone a reductive understanding of the role of the media itself. Blair's comments overtly accept not only that News Limited in general, and *The Australian* in particular, are right-wing, but also that any view running counter to that within the organisation is, legitimately, liable to be quashed. No big deal.

I did seriously think again about quitting, but in the end, I couldn't see the point. Maybe my logic was wrong, but I thought, why should I leave just because some masthead editor has got his nose out of joint over something I wrote? My disappointment was twofold: first, that I wasn't able to post a full explanation of what had happened and thank people for their support; and second, that Chris Mitchell hadn't responded in a different way. The whole approach seemed alien to the values for which good journalism is meant to stand: open debate and a willingness to engage as equals in a democratic society. Swatting away criticism because you can, rather than engaging with it, is ultimately a sign of weakness, not strength.

Strangely enough, though, the story had a happy ending: a couple of years later, Peter Brent, the blogger Mitchell had attacked and whom I'd defended, was invited to move his blog to the website of *The Australian*, under the editorship of Chris Mitchell. Perhaps the logic of my argument had seeped in, but whether it had or not, it was a good outcome. Brent makes a valuable contribution and his blog lends some real credibility to *The Australian*'s polling analysis, a view with which Mitchell obviously concurs.

This was clearly an important moment in the life of *Blogocracy*, but it was hardly the most important. The very existence of the site was a significant innovation in the history of Australia's developing media landscape, but we were always looking for ways to improve what we did. Paul suggested at one stage that I invite a number of bloggers to participate in a series of posts. The idea was that they would each write a piece on a particular topic, to be published on *Blogocracy* and on their own sites, and that we would all link to each other and through news.com.au. It was a way of generating debate as well as building some bridges between the mainstream and both the left and the right wings of the blogosphere. It was a great idea, and although it fizzled a bit in the end, it was definitely worth the effort.

I also invited some guest posts from people with particular expertise as a way of using the site to open up debate on important topics. News.com.au editors were always supportive of this, and so, for instance, in 2007 we had Dr Brigid van Wanrooy write a post about a key piece of research on workplace relations. This was in the run-up to the general election when the Howard government's Work Choices legislation was the hottest topic around, and Dr van Wanrooy wrote an excellent piece and then made herself available to answer questions in comments: precisely the sort of interaction between expert and lay opinion that I thought blogging should make possible. Peter Russo, the lawyer acting on behalf of Mohamed Haneef, the Queensland doctor who was accused by the Howard government of aiding terrorists, also contributed a number of guest posts. The Haneef affair was another huge issue in the run-up to the 2007 election, and it was great to have someone so intimately involved in the matter canvassing the issues at *Blogocracy* and engaging with readers in the comments section. Again, it was an attempt to use the blog to go beyond the sort of interaction that was normally considered possible in the mainstream media.

*Blogocracy*'s real importance, though, I think, was that it provided a left-of-centre voice in a prominent mainstream space. There were any number of right-wing commentators with blogs and columns who consistently and openly supported the Howard government, but *Blogocracy* was the only place in the mainstream where such views were contested and alternatives offered. This made the site not just an aberration within News Limited, but within the broader mainstream media, where Mr Howard had, despite a rocky start to his prime ministership, long since donned an impenetrable Teflon armour. He was seen as somehow uniquely in touch with middle Australia, a political and campaigning savant who, even in his darkest moments, was expected to pull a rabbit out of his hat and win the 2007 election. The attitude is captured beautifully in a cloying quote from senior News Limited journalist and political rock star Paul Kelly: '[John Howard] doesn't have to imagine what ordinary voters think — he has just to decide what he thinks because they are virtually the same.'

I was constantly accused of being biased in the way I discussed the toings and froings of the government, and I guess to some extent I was, but when you consider that not only were Howard and his party very comfortably beaten in the 2007 election but also Howard himself became only the second prime minister in Australian history to lose his own seat, *Blogocracy*'s criticisms of him look a lot less like bias and more like a reflection of the political zeitgeist. That is to say, *Blogocracy* — and the left wing of the blogosphere more generally — was in closer touch with the sentiments of middle Australia than those in the mainstream, who continued to pander to the myth of John Howard's invincibility. I claim no particular insight in this regard, only that the nature of blogging and its interaction with its audience can provide insights that aren't necessarily available to the 'savvy' press gallery.

In the end, the differential between work and reward was such that, towards the end of 2008, I decided to close *Blogocracy*. My remuneration had increased since I started, but it was still a paltry sum. Given the hours I was putting in, it was unsustainable. Nonetheless, I had learned a lot and had appreciated working with such high-calibre people. And I had become more convinced than ever that, if done properly, an active comments facility is a valuable adjunct to the straight journalism that the mainstream provides. But I'd also learned just how hard it is to moderate such a facility and have it operate as a site of genuine democratic give and take. Therein lie the immense promise and practical limitations of the social-media revolution.

## CHAPTER FIVE

# *The Rules of Engagement*

*Dunlop is human garbage.*
BILL CALVIN OF SUNSHINE, IN A COMMENT
ON ANDREW BOLT'S BLOG

A lot of political commentary, whether it is in the mainstream media or on a blog, is, by its nature, confrontational. You can be as civil as you want, but at the end of the day you are expressing an opinion, and that opinion is unlikely to be shared by everyone who reads it. What's more, our entire liberal democracy is predicated on the notion that conflict over personal opinions, sometimes grandly portrayed as the battle of ideas, is essential to democratic equality and governance. Our major institutions, the courts and the parliaments, are proudly described as adversarial, and there are many paeans by politicians, journalists, and even academics praising this kind of confrontation as an intrinsic good. Such confrontation, the argument goes, allows all sides to be heard and the best solutions to emerge.

It is fine to buy into this assertion — and basically, I do — but in so doing, we have to accept the consequences that come with it: arguments are going to arise and they are not always going to be polite. This seems obvious, but given the conniptions that impolite comments threads cause throughout the media, you would think no one had ever thought of it before. I find it incredibly frustrating to still be reading articles such as the one by Bruce Guthrie, former editor of *The Age*, published in May 2013, which begins with the rhetorical question: 'When did public debate in this country degenerate into a tedious game of Chinese whispers?' This posits a time when public debate was of a much higher standard, which begs the question, when was that? The implication of the article, as with so many similar articles, is that this 'degeneration' has occurred because of online comments and social media. Furthermore, in its defence of three prominent figures against name-calling, the article implies that things were better when the only people who could comment were those whom the gatekeepers, the mainstream media, let through.

I am not defending the abuse that occurs online. But I am saying that the constant whining about falling standards of public debate is ahistorical nonsense. It not only ignores the abuse that occurred in the past, but also ignores the fact that back then there was simply nothing comparable to the access that online comments and, more recently, social media afford ordinary people; worst of all, it ignores the fact that comments threads have liberated the voices of large numbers of genuinely articulate and thoughtful people.

The most rewarding but difficult aspect of running *Blogocracy* was moderating the comments section. As the number of participants increased from month to month, moderation took up more and more of my time, to the extent that I often found it overwhelming. It wasn't just the sheer number of comments, though that was obviously part of the difficulty. It was also the matter of maintaining a relationship with people you had never met and were unlikely to meet, of finding ways to respond appropriately to their criticisms and their praise, and carrying on, often at length, what could be difficult discussions about complex and divisive social and political issues. These structural and human limitations to public debate should concern us much more than the constant hand-wringing about the alleged decline in its quality. And indeed, the best way to address the latter is by understanding the former. So let's examine the way in which comment on blogs, and in turn on social media, has developed.

The problem of how to handle comments in the blogosphere has been contentious since the software that allowed readers to comment on posts first came into existence. We all discovered pretty early on that although an active comments section embodied the sort of open discussion most bloggers valued, it could also be a source of irritation, frustration, and outright hostility. Reader comments also had the ability to affect a blog's reputation, and to some extent it didn't matter how measured or careful the tone of your posts was; it was no guarantee that your commenters would take the same approach. A mild-mannered blogger such as Kevin Drum, for instance, who wrote reasonable, fact-filled posts about all aspects of US politics had, at times, a comments section full of vitriol and spite, almost in inverse proportion to his own good-humoured reasonableness.

We should remember, too, that it would be wrong to conclude that all blogs discouraged abusive comments. Some were loath to moderate their comments section because of an ideological commitment to free speech, a view wherein any interference with what someone said was seen as undesirable. Of the early Australian blogs, *Catallaxy* is probably the classic example of this. The blog's founder, Jason Soon, another in the Kevin Drum mould (though elsewhere on the political spectrum), was a measured polemicist, but his hands-off approach to moderation allowed the site's comments section to become legendary for its ill-tempered, intemperate abuse — a reputation it maintains to this day, especially now that the site has many more contributors who lack Soon's reserve and decency.

Other sites went out of their way to encourage abusive comments — as long as they were directed at the blog's ideological enemies — and this became another aspect of the role of commenters: they were deployed as a weapon against those who disagreed with the views expressed by the blogger. I don't think even too many on the right would dispute the contention that it was right-wing blogs, the so-called attack blogs, who refined and harnessed this particular form of intimidation; it was well known in the blogosphere that if you wrote a post that for whatever reason raised the always-primed ire of certain right-wing bloggers and their audience, your comments box was liable to fill up with abuse. The practice became so widespread that it developed its own nomenclature, and terms such as 'trolling' and 'right-wing death beasts' gained currency.

The truth is, in the early days most of the blogosphere, like the internet more generally, was dedicated to propositions of openness. The origins of this attitude are well documented, but the idea was sometimes taken to extremes. The promotion of 'openness' took on an aura of religious fervour, and there is no doubt that a commitment to the concept pervaded every aspect of online interaction. The whole architecture of blogging, built as it was on the practice of linking, presupposed the existence of freely available articles that could be linked to and talked about. No wonder the majority of us absorbed notions of openness so easily — almost uncritically. Indeed, Google itself, that Otis elevator of the online world, relied on being able to seek and find and make available information that people could easily access and read for free. This is the crux of the entire disruptive power of the world wide web: the fact that it created a virtual space of free exchange in a world that has long been in thrall to the power of competitive, commercial markets.

The internet affected (and is still affecting) all sorts of industries, but the people who bore the early brunt of it were the music, book, and media corporations. It was their products that were most easily digitised, and for which there existed an almost bottomless pit of producers who were able to oversupply pre-existing markets. The fact that many of these producers didn't see themselves as producers in a commercial sense, and were therefore willing to create and curate content for no remuneration at all, merely added to the problems of the legacy industries. This is why media executives such as Rupert Murdoch of News Corporation and Tom Curley of the Associated Press started accusing companies such as Google of stealing their product. 'We content creators have been too slow to react to the free exploitation of news by third parties without input or permission,' Curley said at a meeting of media executives in Beijing in 2009. Murdoch told the same audience: 'The aggregators and plagiarists will soon have to pay a price for the co-opting of our content. But if we do not take advantage of the current movement toward paid content, it will be the content creators — the people in this hall — who will pay the ultimate price and the content kleptomaniacs who triumph.'

An element of the disruption I'm talking about is, obviously, commercial. But a big part of it was also that the technology empowered individuals at the expense of established gatekeepers, and it provided the means of aggregating those individuals into a network of content creators and consumers who no longer relied on the choices made by others — whether they be book and newspaper editors or the A&R guys at music labels. It empowered users and gave them the sense that they were now autonomous in the public sphere in a way they never had been before. Yes, that power is likely more circumscribed than many people thought in those early days, but at least initially, the experience of using the web to discuss politics felt revolutionary and anti-establishment. It put individuals in touch with others who were thinking about the same things they were. It is often argued that in the process people were ghettoised into partisan camps that became echo chambers of the like-minded, but I would dispute this. At least at first, the empowerment people commenting on blogs felt arose because they were suddenly in an environment where they could talk about topics that interested them in an open and unrestricted way at a time of their own choosing. The partisan leanings of those they encountered just made the whole process more interesting. The reaction was something like, Wow, there are people out there who really think like *that*?

These issues of openness, engagement, and civility were at the forefront of my thinking when I started blogging for News Limited. When I wrote in my opening post for *Blogocracy* that the idea was 'to pick apart the issues of the day in the way that normal human beings talk about such things', it wasn't just some pose designed to assert my 'ordinary Joe' credentials, but a considered approach to public debate that aimed to be as inclusive as possible. I wanted to discuss serious matters with my readers, but I didn't want the site to turn into an academic conference. I didn't want to dumb things down, either. I just wanted people to feel comfortable speaking in their own voice, and if it meant allowing a certain level of robustness, I was fine with that. It was an Orwellian approach — but in the good sense of that term! Orwell's great legacy is the attention he gave to political writing and his commitment to plain speech. In his essay 'Politics and the English Language', he wrote:

> The defence of the English language ... has nothing to do with archaism, with the salvaging of obsolete words and turns of speech, or with the setting up of a 'standard English' which must never be departed from. On the contrary, it is especially concerned with the scrapping of every word or idiom which has outworn its usefulness. It has nothing to do with correct grammar and syntax, which are of no importance so long as one makes one's meaning clear, or with the avoidance of Americanisms, or with having what is called a 'good prose style'.

I shared that view — and God spare me from the pedants and grammar Nazis who spring up online to piously correct every misplaced comma and colloquial turn of phrase.

The one proviso I put on our interactions at *Blogocracy* was also noted in my first post: 'The only other thing to say about comments is to keep it all reasonably polite or the whole thing won't work.'

This was a nice sentiment, but in practice the lines between acceptable and unacceptable behaviour are much harder to draw. What's more, drawing them, enforcing a standard and applying it consistently, is time-consuming and intensive. You set yourself up as the sole arbitrator of any disputes that arise, and the discussion about such arbitration can be the most divisive and distracting interaction you have online — and I'm not the only one to realise this. The formal guidelines that gradually evolved at the popular group blog *Larvatus Prodeo* included the statement: 'No public discussion will be entered into regarding moderation decisions. If readers or commenters have queries about this policy, they may email the site or its contributors.' Unfortunately it took me a long while to realise the value of such a rule, and way too much of my time was spent going back and forth with people who wanted to challenge a 'ruling' instead of continuing with the conversation at hand. (You could even argue, I think, that this is the fundamental weakness of Twitter, that it is defenceless against that sort of endless meta-conversation, where people constantly argue not about a given issue, but about how people are responding to it.)

Right from the beginning, the problems that arose in moderating comments at *Blogocracy* were often to do with finding the right equilibrium. I wanted people to be free to make playful comments, make jokes at my expense or at the expense of others, and sometimes descend, jokingly or sarcastically, into the realms of bad language. But when they did, I had to balance those comments against similar comments employing similar language that, for whatever reason, just didn't work as humour and thus crossed the line and became offensive. It is almost impossible to allow one person's smart-arse comment that mocks somebody-or-other, and then disallow someone else's comment because they are being rude. No matter how obvious the difference is between the tone of the two comments, not everyone, and especially not the author of the banned comment, will accept your interpretation. A comments box lacks the nuances of face-to-face speech, and it is probably fair to say that a playful tone is the first casualty of online discussions in most blogs; I didn't want that to be the case with mine.

The other key difficulty of moderation is time. When I was running *Blogocracy*, I started work early every morning and had a post up by no later than 7.00 a.m. so that it could be ready and waiting when the first big wave of readers came online over their breakfast. But even as I was writing that first post, I was also flitting back and forth to the comments moderation page, reading comments that had come in overnight and approving them so that they appeared on site. I was always extremely conscious that the sort of interaction with readers that I valued in blogging relied on making the gap between commenting and the appearance of the comment on the site as brief as possible. People got genuinely upset if their contribution didn't show up quickly enough. Indeed, I was constantly fielding emails from people asking why their comment hadn't appeared yet. The reality was that there were many reasons why it might sometimes take a while, not least being that I was either eating or sleeping. But by and large I kept the queue flowing at a decent clip.

Once my first post of the day was up, I would immediately start work on the next, and continue this process throughout the day. At the same time, comments were flowing in, and I was in and out of the moderation queue, approving them and, as often as possible, responding to them. By that, I don't mean that I tried to respond to everyone (that would have been impossible and probably lethal); I just responded as regularly as I could and in a way, I hoped, that encouraged further conversation. I'd normally get my final post for the day up by about 3.00 p.m. and then the rest of my working day would be spent replying to comments and a steady stream of emails from readers. The flow of both never stopped.

The time involved in the moderation process was obvious to the editors at News Interactive; they were certainly aware of similar issues affecting Andrew Bolt. He had built a thriving community of engaged and enthusiastic readers at his *Herald Sun* site, and he, too, was finding it more and more difficult to keep up. In order to help him out, the company employed moderators, people who took charge of his comments section, handling the day-to-day job of deciding what would be posted on the site and what wouldn't. It was a perfectly legitimate solution to a growing problem, and I mean no criticism when I say that, when I was offered moderators of my own, I turned them down.

My background in the independent blogosphere played a big part in that decision. I was still committed to the idea of the blog as a site for conversation. I wanted the readership to be as wide and as deep as possible, and my hope in going to News Limited was that the largest media company in the country would provide me with access to that wider audience. It was all about a belief in the importance of society having places where people could come together as equals and discuss matters of social and political importance. My role, the role of anyone who ran a blog, was to act as a host for these discussions, to be the person who not only wrote the posts to which people responded, but who was present in the comments section, distributing the liquor of encouragement in the form of praise and thanks and sometimes pushback. I really didn't care if people criticised me, as long as what they said was factual and temperate. As I said in an email exchange with Paul Colgan: 'I'm inclined to let stupid swipes at me through, and more inclined to pull those that abuse other commenters. Basically, though, I'm pretty pleased that the site has built up a sturdy group of conservative commenters who are willing to take me to task on just about everything.' The main thing, as far as I was concerned, was that a given topic got a decent airing and — this was the real dream — that those opinions somehow formed part of the conversation that those in power took note of when making decisions about the running of the country. To put it simply, I wanted my readers not just to talk, but also to be heard. So the idea that I would hand over control of the comments section to moderators was completely at odds with what I had set out to do.

I explained this to the editors and they were more than happy to accept my decision. I kept full responsibility for the comments section, the only problem being that no human could maintain that sort of pace indefinitely.

It wasn't just a matter of numbers; it was a matter of intensity. With the best will in the world, it is pretty hard to keep up a meaningful relationship with hundreds of people and do justice to their involvement. There are those who argue that an online relationship is not real, that it is almost by definition an inferior way to know someone given that you never actually meet the person in the flesh, but this is a very narrow understanding of what it means to 'know' someone. When you speak with them every day, discuss matters that go to the heart of the democratic life of the nation, and hear their views on all sorts of topics, it is pretty hard to argue that that is not a close, almost intimate relationship. It is certainly real, as is the pressure that builds on the moderator.

One way of managing this intensity is to introduce topics of conversation that are less fraught, less likely to evoke the sort of deep, character-forming views that are part and parcel of social and political issues. *Blogocracy*, like many other blogs, did this. I had regular spots on Wednesday and Friday where I threw the comments section open to any topic that people wanted to discuss, from what they had for dinner to what music they were listening to. We talked about sport and films and books and holidays and our families, and even exchanged recipes. Such conversations tended to be less confrontational than ones about politics, naturally enough, and they also had the effect of providing some common ground between people who argued with each other, sometimes heatedly, about politics. They were a release valve for me, too, and I hope that those involved enjoyed them as much as I did.

Of course, if all commenters were just one big happy family of rational citizens freely and openly exchanging ideas in an atmosphere of equality and mutual respect, the issue of comment moderation would never have become such a hot topic. Clearly they are not, and so at some point everyone who runs a site that invites comments is going to have to deal with abuse, incivility, disagreement, and other forms of confrontation.

The times when I disallowed a comment were pretty rare, which is quite remarkable given the number of comments that were coming through. You really had to be very offensive or, more likely, to have strayed over into actual libel, for me to bring down the guillotine. This occasionally happened when a topic arose that involved a court case, and in those situations I was happy to be able to seek advice from the News Limited legal department.

Having access to such expertise was one of the clear advantages of working for a big media company, and really did relieve the pressure of dealing with potentially problematic comments.

The times I actually banned commenters were even less common. On a couple of occasions I put one or two people on a two-week ban, and there were a few other times I strongly urged people to get their act together before I would allow them to continue commenting, but that was about it. I think there was only one person I banned outright in more than two years at *Blogocracy*.

In retrospect, though, I probably got the balance wrong. I really believed that it was possible for abusive commenters, once they had got some anger off their chests, to turn into useful contributors, and this was certainly my experience. But overall, I think I was far too forgiving, and that some comments threads suffered because of it. Any community needs structure, and in trying to be as open as possible, I wasn't providing that structure as effectively as I could have been. It is all very well to play the long game with abusive commenters and perhaps encourage them to change their ways, but in the meantime you are probably creating an environment that many others find too hostile to enter. Thus, we reach the libertarian's dilemma: you can feel all superior and gooey about your commitment to unregulated free speech, but the very lack of regulation only serves to undermine the freedom of less aggressive or less confident members of the community and scare them off. In addition, the long game takes time and energy and patience, and as I have pointed out, you don't always have those things in reserve when you are blogging — at least when the blog has serious traffic. A little more structure from the beginning would have not just helped the conversation but, over time, saved me a lot of work.

Another mistake I made was not enforcing a strict word limit. Keeping comments to, say, 300 words would have saved me reading time, and also would've forced some discipline on those commenters who were inclined to get a bit carried away. As it was, I regularly had comments that exceeded 1000 words, and you don't need too many of them in a day before it becomes burdensome. The reason I rarely enforced a limit was, again, because of a commitment to giving readers as much freedom as possible to express their views. It reminds me of a quote attributed to Winston Churchill, which goes something like, 'I'm sorry this is such a long letter, I didn't have time to write a short one.' There is certainly something to be said for encouraging people to hone in on exactly what they want to say. In fact, adhering to a strict word limit is one of the disciplines of journalism itself — as well as the key to understanding the contemporary success of Twitter. Less really can be more in the online environment, where traditional notions of space don't apply.

Yet for all its problems, running a thriving comments section was a genuinely gratifying experience. My regrets have nothing to do with the commenters themselves, just with the fact that in hindsight I realise I could have offered a better service and, in the process, saved myself some grief. Too much of the public discussion about comments threads accentuates the negative, and we really need to move past this mindset; apart from anything else, a good comments community can become self-policing, and your own readers become the best protection you have against unacceptable behaviour. Many of those in the old media and other traditional locations of power in our society, people such as politicians and business leaders, who suddenly find themselves on the receiving end of online abuse, fail to understand this, and are way too eager to yell that the sky is falling. As Anthony Barnett from *openDemocracy* has argued:

> The debate that matters about the web and social media is taking place on the web itself and within its social networks. It is about standards, openness, protocols, integrity and trust as well as innovation, exposure and investigation. The problem with outside critics is that they don't see the web as the home of the extraordinary learning experience that it is.

*Blogocracy* definitely benefited from such a self-regulating community.

I also suspect that I am not alone in my experience: that most long-term bloggers have had something of a change of heart over their ideas about commenting. The commitment to open debate is still there, but the approach to achieving it has changed from one of complete openness to one of well-managed interaction that encourages the community itself to maintain workable standards.

There was no single moment when things changed, and indeed, there is still no clear view on how best to address the issue of comment moderation. My sense is that the independent blogosphere was the incubator for various new approaches to readers' comments, and this was partly the result of access to better technology, as blogging software developed better tools for moderation. It might also have been a by-product of a simple lack of resources. Amateurs, blogging in their spare time, didn't have the time or money to deal with increasing numbers of commenters, and so were more or less forced into imposing some limits.

One of the first Australian bloggers to realise the importance of providing a stricter framework for comments was John Quiggin, who very early on introduced a no-swearing rule, and has since beefed up his comments regime by enforcing bans on certain topics of conversation while having a fairly robust policy of putting commenters into a moderation queue rather than allowing them to post directly to the site itself. John also runs a regular Monday open thread, where people can talk on any topic, as well as a weekend reflection thread, where people can talk at greater length about the topics they choose. In late 2010, he introduced another open thread that he calls the Sandpit, which he explained in this way:

I've been dissatisfied with the way comments threads have been going for a while, in particular because I feel that they rapidly become dialogues (or competing monologues) involving a small group of regulars. That discourages new commenters from joining in. So, I'm establishing this sandpit post, as a venue for any lengthy discussions that arise, particularly if they are off the original topic. The comments policy regarding civil discussion still applies, but I'll try to be reasonably lighthanded.

So, my request is that commenters avoid lengthy interchanges on the main comments threads, and take these to the sandpit, where they can debate to their heart's content. I'll issue requests along these lines, if necessary, but I'd rather not. I may also impose, or reimpose one comment/thread/day limits on individual commenters to keep things under control. With that said, fire away.

The strength of this approach is not only that it sets out clearly the standards that are expected, but also that it does so in a way that presumes most participants will be adults who can be relied upon to do the right thing of their own accord — while also allowing for the fact that, as in any public space, there will be drongos who want to stir things up. John is saying, Come into my house, by all means, but understand that there are rules, and if you break them, there will be sanctions.

Given the amount of abuse directed at the blogosphere by the mainstream media, it is perhaps ironic that some of the least regulated and ultimately unedifying public comments threads still occur on their sites. There are exceptions, but they tend to prove the rule. One genuine exception is former News Limited columnist George Megalogenis, who made a concerted effort to enforce standards on his blog at *The Australian*. This was so successful that by the time he left the job he was able to say, 'Thank you to everyone here who made this blog one of the most enjoyable parts of my career. I learnt more in our exchanges over the past five years than in any background briefing from prime ministers or treasurers.'

Inadequately moderated comment communities are still too common in the mainstream media, and there are bloggers and columnists who still seem to get a kick out of stirring up discontent for its own sake. When Piers Akerman, for example, writes a post on his *Telegraph* blog that begins, 'The hand-flapping hysteria generated by the planned removal of the rainbow-coloured Taylor Square crosswalk is symptomatic of a politically correct push by the noisy end of the homosexual lobby to inflict its narrow agenda on the broader community', you can guarantee that the comments will include a reasonable number of references to 'poofters' and 'perversion'; and sure enough, they are there, if you have the stomach to wade through them. (Mr Akerman, of course, is not a 'troll' or a 'symptom of the decline of the standards of public debate', the usual accusations thrown at bloggers and other users of social media. He is, in the language of his profession, a 'hard-hitting journalist', and that makes it okay for him to bait his audience.)

But the problem is not limited to the tabloid sites. Even the comments threads at ABC Online's *The Drum*, for example, can vary wildly in terms of quality. The issue at all of these sites is not necessarily incivility so much as it is off-topic diversions that undermine the idea of meaningful discussion. Partly this is attributable to the time it takes to moderate comments, and we should never underestimate that. But I wonder if the habit of using the number of comments on a thread as a metric of success has contributed to the problem. There is definitely a temptation to let questionable comments through simply because it boosts numbers. It might be time to kill the comment counters and let moderators focus on the comments themselves.

Overall, though, I would say things are improving. Mainstream sites have instigated new approaches that try to keep the discussion more focused and the lines of communication open. *The New York Times* has been at the forefront of some of these innovations, being among the first sites to introduce 'threaded' commenting (whereby commenters can respond directly to other comments and create a sub-discussion within the overall conversation), as well as introducing the idea of a 'trusted commenter'. Under this system, once you achieve trusted status, certain advantages accrue — most specifically, your comments go straight to site and avoid the moderation queue. The paper is also experimenting with a system where readers are asked to define their position on a given story (positive, negative, surprised, unsurprised) before commenting, and they are limited to a 100-word response. The idea is to frame responses more narrowly and thus encourage much more specific discussion. I'm all for this sort of experimentation.

The Australian site Newsflock (still in an early phase of development as I write this) is using a comments promotion system whereby readers can vote comments up or down, and thus help to guide the conversation. Better and more relevant comments rise higher in the thread, while abuse and nonsense is relegated to a less prominent position. The same can be done with articles themselves, and so the community involved in Newsflock are actively creating a 'front page' that reflects their interests.

Even a site such as *Gawker*, which specialises in an irreverent and even confrontational approach to the news, is constantly tweaking its approach to comments in order to manage them better. *Gawker*'s most recent update allows commenters to accept or dismiss replies to their own comments by clicking on the appropriate buttons. In this way, readers are able to maintain some quality control over the conversation in which they are participating. The system also allows readers to isolate a particular thread within the overall post and link directly to that thread via various forms of social media.

*Gawker* realises that their community is not just the heart and soul of what they do but also the key to their financial success. And maybe this is the route to reform:

once mainstream media organisations stop looking at comments sections as a problem to be managed and instead treat them as a resource to be cultivated, they will decide it is worth putting more effort into meaningful moderation.

With the rise of social media, it is clear that the nature of online commentary has changed considerably since those early days of blogging. While once media companies only had to worry about moderating commenters, today people are just as likely to use Twitter and Facebook and other social-media sites and communities to record their reactions to an article or a post as they are to use the comments box under the piece itself. This has not only multiplied the fronts on which journalists might be expected to engage with their readers; it has made the journalists themselves the front-counter staff in the retail relationship they increasingly have with their customers.

On the whole, I think social media is a good thing; I'm a fan. Though whether it is good or bad is to some extent beside the point: it simply is, and people, particularly journalists, should spend less time bemoaning the public's involvement in it and more time finding ways to make it work better. They especially need to realise that once you commit to social media, you have to *engage*. You cannot put out the welcome mat in the form of a Facebook page and a Twitter account but ignore comments when they come.

The approach PolitiFact Australia took in a recent exchange over one of their posts is a good example of how having a pretty website with all the bells and whistles of social media isn't enough if you don't engage with those who use these platforms. PolitiFact Australia is a site that checks various claims made by politicians. It then makes a 'ruling', as it's called, about the veracity of those claims. During the week of its launch, in May 2013, a claim made by the Labor Party, that 'its workplace rights can't be stripped away', was ruled to be 'false'. Twitter lit up with people pointing out that PolitiFact had misunderstood the nature of the claim. PolitiFact argued that the claim was false because a future government could change the law and therefore people's workplace rights could be stripped away. Their interlocutors on Twitter and various blogs replied that what Labor was actually claiming was that their laws meant *employers*, not a future government, were prevented from stripping rights away. This was so obvious that it is surprising PolitiFact even argued the toss. But argue they did, and in a way that showed a complete contempt for their critics. Rather than engaging with them individually as their comments came up on Twitter, PolitiFact took to their Facebook page and wrote a generalised response, reasserting the correctness of their original ruling. The only use they made of Twitter was to announce that they had written a response on their Facebook page. And the original 'ruling' published on their website remains, at the time of publication, unchanged, completely failing to acknowledge the very reasonable alternative interpretation offered by their readers.

If you want to know why sometimes things get heated

on social media, this is part of the explanation. It is because those with relative power create a presence on social media and therefore enter into a social contract to engage as equals with their followers. But when a matter arises that calls for engagement, they instead retreat, treat all comments as hostile fire, and assert their superiority. This is a very old-media reaction, and it is not surprising to discover that PolitiFact Australia is run by a former editor-in-chief of *The Sunday Age* and publisher of the *Sun Herald* — in other words, someone from the heartland of the gatekeeper media.

My point is not just to criticise PolitiFact. To some extent we are all, audience and media alike, still struggling to work out how to behave in this new environment. In fact, there will never be hard and fast rules of engagement, only an ongoing debate about what works and what doesn't work in a given situation. And that is precisely why we need to talk to each other about our expectations. In old media, journalists and editors could pull up the drawbridge. With new media, they're in the moat with everyone else.

In my experience, successful and long-term exponents of online commentary, and of new media, don't get too bothered about abusive commenters. Obviously they find them deplorable, but it is not a sore that constantly needs to be picked at. I think we have to be careful not to overreact and use the bad behaviour of the few as a way of condemning online conversations in general. Nonetheless, if you are going to invite public participation, it is essential to put in place some rules in order to deal with it and then enforce them as consistently as you can. If you want to encourage meaningful interaction within a community, you have to provide a safe place for that to happen.

But here is the hard truth for those of us who champion the interactive nature of new media: it may simply be impossible for a working journalist to do his or her job properly while also engaging with readers in the way that blogging — and now social media, especially Twitter — suggests is ideal. If that is the case, then many of us have to rethink our stance. Media organisations need to realise that yes, people want to have their say, but they are not so foolish that they don't understand the limitations of what is possible.

Given all this, there is no substitute for respect for readers (for heaven's sake, stop writing articles about how rude and stupid people on social media are!) and for transparency about the rules. Create a welcoming environment where people feel safe to express their views and where they feel that their contribution is valued, and you go a long way to marginalising the sort of abuse that does occur. What's more, if you create a presence on social media, you have to be willing to speak to those who speak to you. You don't have to respond to everyone, but you cannot take the PolitiFact approach of raising the drawbridge.

Commenters, and those who speak to you via social media, are not the enemy; they are the audience.

## CHAPTER SIX

# The Great Troll Wars

*What if this was the worst political reporting Australians have endured in history? Dysfunctional, with lousy judgment, fixated with polls, feigning concern about the toxicity of political discourse.*

GAY ALCORN, FORMER EDITOR OF THE SUNDAY AGE

'Trolling' is a word that reaches back deep into the early days of the internet, to a time before the rise of blogging and comments threads. The fact that online communities, even in those early days, needed the word suggests that the behaviour it describes was fairly prevalent.

I must admit, I laughed the first time I heard the expression, back in the *Surfdom* days. Once comments boxes became common, the term suddenly seemed to be everywhere, along with descriptors such as 'right-wing death beasts' and 'attack blogs'. That all of these expressions have a vaguely medieval, or even fantasy, feel to them, might also tell us something about the geekish mindset that tended to predominate in online communities.

But what are we talking about when we talk about 'trolls' and 'trolling'? Wikipedia says, 'In Old Norse sources, beings described as trolls dwell in isolated rocks, mountains, or caves, live together in small family units, and are rarely helpful to human beings.' In internet parlance, a troll is a lurker, a generally anonymous person who frequents a given site and waits for the opportunity to intervene in a comments thread. Internet trolls, according to Wikipedia, '[post] inflammatory, extraneous, or off-topic messages in an online community, such as a forum, chat room, or blog, with the primary intent of provoking readers into an emotional response or of otherwise disrupting normal on-topic discussion'. They, too, are rarely helpful to human beings.

Despite this well-established usage, the term has come to mean something far less specific in recent years.

The mainstream media today uses 'trolling' to describe virtually any form of online behaviour that they deem offensive or unacceptable. The shift in emphasis from specifically disruptive and provocative behaviour to a much more general idea of *uncivil* behaviour is significant. In media usage, the meaning of the word is now so broad that everything from the odd use of swear words to overt threats to do someone physical harm is 'trolling'; it has ceased to be a useful descriptive term and has entered the realm of cliché.

This redefinition and descent into meaninglessness has not gone unchallenged, but the battle to keep a precise and narrow meaning for the word has been lost. The mainstream media's ability to redefine it in this way — by basically using it as a catch-all term to describe any online behaviour they don't like — is a reflection of their societal power, and any discussion about internet trolling is, at root, about the exercise of that power.

So it is surprising how often the power imbalance between commentators and commenters — between the media and their audience — is overlooked. Most journalists don't see themselves as particularly powerful, and their work is constrained by the input of editors and subeditors, and ultimately proprietors and other managers; but the simple truth, as we've discussed, is that even as they work within these constraints, they are able to inject their words and their thoughts into the public sphere via prestigious and powerful institutions, which puts them at an enormous advantage relative to the average citizen. A given journalist may or may not be part of the elite, per se, but they are definitely operating in an elite environment, where they are accorded certain privileges not available to most of their audience.

Those who ignore the lines of power in online discussion offer a range of self-serving explanations for trolling behaviour, and these tend to hone in on a couple of supposed causes. Anonymity has become the favoured one, the idea being that the ability to hide behind a false identity when commenting divorces people from the self-restraint that usually governs their interactions with others. The alternative theory is that trolls are just stupid, or ill mannered, or ignorant, a logic that is less analytical than it is designed to flatter the person making the accusation. Search the plethora of articles about trolling, and again and again these two explanations arise.

Both are unsatisfactory. Don't get me wrong: there

is certainly a band of trolls who purposefully set out to disrupt online discussion for the sake of it, or simply decide to abuse certain people, and no doubt some of them of are stupid, ignorant, misogynistic, and ill mannered. But I suspect they are a minority. Certainly in my experience at *Blogocracy* they were, and in some ways they were also the easiest to control — at least once I accepted that warning someone, or banning them from a comments thread, was a reasonable thing to do. However, without considering the power relationships that exist in various online discussions, we will never understand trolling; anonymity, stupidity, and bad manners are inadequate explanations of a more complex phenomenon.

So let's look at some of the more prominent reactions to what those in the media call 'trolling'.

In September 2012 Sydney's *Telegraph* ran a 'campaign' against trolling, beginning with an online petition and series of articles in the paper. The campaign was largely a response to a number of high-profile attacks on various people within the media — or perhaps I should say, a number of attacks on high-profile people within the media. In particular, it seems to have been prompted by what was described as a 'hate campaign' against television personality Charlotte Dawson.

The opening paragraph of the petition reads as follows: 'This is a *Daily Telegraph* (Sydney) and www.TheTelegraph.com.au petition to stop the vile and abusive trolls on Twitter that facelessly and mercilessly attack not just celebrities and sports stars but other everyday users simply for the thrill.' The accompanying article, written by journalist Gemma Jones, expresses similar concerns about trolling on Twitter. Under the headline 'Time Is Up for Twitter Trolls and Bullies', and illustrated with images of two high-profile sports stars and Dawson herself, the article wastes no time in unveiling threats and in invoking the use of state power: 'Today we launch a campaign to stand up to the faceless bullies and to urge Twitter to unmask them and turn them in to authorities so they can be prosecuted.' A number of sports stars, including the Australian cricket captain, are quoted in support, as are media personalities, and, somewhat hilariously, radio presenter Ray Hadley. (Hadley, whose use of intemperate language and hyperbole to attack enemies and fire up listeners is similar to the stock-in-trade of many shock jocks, apparently followed the *Telegraph*'s lead by 'speaking out against abusers' on his radio show. So unlikely a champion of civility is Hadley that the article includes a tweet from federal MP Mike Kelly highlighting this fact: 'An airwaves troll trolling the digital trollers. We've come full circle.')

Although the *Telegraph* paid a certain amount of attention to ordinary victims of trolling, the paper's interest was inflected with elite concerns from the get-go. It is fair to say that if the object of the trolls' ire had been limited to unknown people using social media, no petition would have been launched. The campaign is thus part of the promotion of celebrity culture that is the bread and butter of most tabloid media. As is typical of this sort of sensationalist campaigning, the issue was dressed up in portentous language and made to sound like an earth-shattering problem. It was also directed specifically at Twitter, a manoeuvre that allowed the *Telegraph* to overlook any similar issues on their own site, let alone other sites under the News Limited banner, and enabled them to single out a company that has become something of a competitor. The net effect was to represent ordinary people as perpetrators of trolling, and members of various elites — journalists, celebrities, sports stars, and even politicians — as its victims.

The focus on anonymity is connected to this idea. Anonymity becomes a marker not just of cowardice and deception, but also of status. You cannot be an anonymous celebrity or politician or business leader or journalist; anonymity marks you as a pleb. It strips people of their status. So the cultural gatekeepers who complain about trolling also consistently complain about anonymity, often suggesting that the cure for trolling is simply to ban anonymity; but the logic behind this demand is less to do with wanting a more 'honest' debate than with the fact that once someone's identity is exposed, the advantage tips to the person with the higher profile, the higher social status.

You can see this equation at work in comments such as those made by union leader Paul Howes in a piece published, not coincidentally, in the *Telegraph* in November 2010. Defending retiring New South Wales

Labor politician Joe Tripodi against online 'attacks', Howes writes:

> When he announced his resignation, some of the comments made on the subsequent news story were pretty brutal. They ranged from your garden-variety slur — 'good riddance to bad rubbish' through to 'gutless muppet', and to the nastiest I read, 'incompetent corrupt clown'.
>
> And so while Joe Tripodi did have his fair share of ups and downs during his time in State Parliament, I think we need to start having a good hard look at what the 'new media' is doing to our political discourse.
>
> In my recent book, *Confessions of a Faceless Man*, I dish out plenty of criticisms against lots of people. But I put my name to it. And it went through a number of lawyers first. I didn't do it from behind my computer screen, basking in my own anonymity.
>
> However, websites like Twitter, and news sites which encourage readers comments, are making it easier than ever before for the deranged and the insane (and rarely, the completely lucid) to say whatever they like about whoever they want.

So notice: a union leader and Labor Party kingmaker is very concerned that another Labor Party heavyweight, a former state minister, and person that *The Sydney Morning Herald* describes as having 'been responsible for the downfall of premiers Morris Iemma and his successor Nathan

Rees', has been attacked by anonymous people on a social-media site. Howes is given space in the largest circulation newspaper in the country, owned by the biggest media organisation in the world, to decry the terrible things that a handful of ordinary people have called his friend. In listing his concerns, he ticks the anonymity box and goes out of his way to note that he, too, 'dishes out plenty of criticisms' but does it under his own name. From all this he concludes not just that some people are mean, but also that there might in fact be something seriously wrong with this whole idea of letting people speak freely on social media, especially under an assumed identity. The article is like a Rosetta Stone of elite concerns about ordinary people entering the public sphere, revealing all the prejudices and values that tend to inform this debate as it is constructed by the mainstream media and by 'victims' such as Howes:

> Simply put, we don't much like people who think they're better than us, and we don't much like politicians, because we think they think they're better than us.
>
> They think they can tell us what to do. They think they can swan around with big pensions and big salaries, and we think most of them wouldn't know hard work if they fell over it.
>
> It's not true, of course. Most parliamentarians, on both sides, work hard, gruelling hours. They do things that normal people wouldn't dream of doing, like flying to Perth, landing at 6am, going to a full day of meetings, then flying home again.

All this denigration of ordinary people because someone on a website called his friend, a former Labor Party powerbroker, a 'gutless muppet'!

Two years later, the *Telegraph*'s anti-trolling initiative proceeded along similar lines. Perhaps what is most astounding about the way the 'campaign' was framed is that Gemma Jones' article made great play of it having the support of a number of senior federal politicians. The mere fact that we are dealing with an organisation that could get former (and future) prime minister Kevin Rudd; the federal treasurer, Wayne Swan; and the nation's leading law officer, attorney-general Nicola Roxon, to go on the record in support of what is essentially an attack on free speech gives some idea of the power differential at work here. Roxon, for instance, is quoted as saying, 'What we need is strong co-operation from governments, law enforcement and the community. But we also need the assistance of US-based social networks.'

To its credit, an editorial in the *Telegraph* on the same day did a better job of wrestling with the issues involved, and at least made some attempt to focus on the most egregious sort of abuse that shows up on Twitter. But in so doing, it emphasised another aspect of the campaign against trolling — namely, that this is also a battle between new media and old.

The editorialists are at pains to draw a distinction between what they see as their legitimate pursuit of free speech and the illegitimate use of free speech by others on social media:

*The Daily Telegraph* and our parent company have long campaigned for increased freedom of speech. Part of this has been to respectfully disagree with moves that would increase government regulation of the media ...

At the same time some seek further regulation, advances in electronic media provide ever-expanding opportunities for those who wish to engage with traditional press outlets.

There is no shortage of fact-checkers among our readers, both online and in our letters pages.

Yet the freedom to engage via electronic media is clearly being abused by those anonymous cowards who use Twitter and other social media platforms simply to increase Australia's stocks of misery and distress.

And it is being done without any means of correction available to those who are targeted.

Most people familiar with the standards of the tabloid media would be tempted to laugh at this assertion of the moral high ground. The writers' obvious discomfort over the rise of 'ever-expanding opportunities' for their audience to engage with and fact-check their work is also revealing; it puts the issue of policing trolls into the context of the paper's self-assumed role as a gatekeeper.

Given such examples, it would not be going too far to suggest that the campaign against trolls is at least partly driven by the mainstream media's anxiety at having lost ground to social media and thus to the audience itself. This is a turf war.

When mainstream-media figures engage in the same sort of behaviour as trolls — when Piers Akerman baits readers on issues like gay marriage, or Miranda Devine unleashes on feminists — they are cut slack that simply isn't afforded to members of the public on social media. A mainstream-media organisation genuinely motivated to clean up public speech would begin by getting its own house in order, not focus on ways to increase regulation of social media while insisting on its own right to remain as unregulated as possible.

Another way of looking at the anti-trolling campaign — both the one launched by the *Telegraph* and the more general one that has become a regular point of discussion in the media — is provided by academic Jason Wilson. He sees it as an example of moral panic, and as he explains on his blog:

> The term 'moral panic' denotes a peculiarly modern confluence of mass mediated anxiety, social deviance and state authority which periodically sweeps contemporary western cultures. What we're witnessing now has many of the features that sociologists noted in coining the term in the 1970s. In 1972 Stanley Cohen had already named as 'folk devils' those individuals, groups or things at the centre of panics, who were defined as presenting an existential threat to the social order. 'Moral entrepreneurs' were the folk who mobilised the media and the people at large in the defence of allegedly threatened moral values. Back in the 70s politicians

and community-based crusaders usually filled this position.

... Moral panics featured *concern* about someone or something deemed likely to have a negative impact on society; *hostility* to that someone or something — enough to turn them into folk devils; the development of a *consensus* driven by the media and moral entrepreneurs that the folk devils in question do represent a problem; action being taken which was *disproportionate* to the threat, and *volatility*, which describes the aptness with which panics are likely to disappear or change in focus.

The *Telegraph*'s petition fits almost exactly the definition of a moral panic. But Wilson also notes that this is a panic driven by the media in particular. He observes: 'It's no surprise to find journalists ... becoming anxious about technologies and practices that threaten a diminishment of their skills, and their role' and that 'Trolling has blown up into a media anxiety because it is a living reminder of the way in which technology has reduced journalists' capacity for controlling the parameters of public debate.'

The media redefinition of trolling, turning it into a much more general term used to mean almost any sort of behaviour centred on bad language, personal abuse, and criticism conducted from behind a cloak of anonymity, has the effect of making the media itself — or the high-profile individuals and celebrities it enlists — the final arbiter of acceptable and unacceptable behaviour online. The moral panic it provokes is designed to serve the status quo and thus reinforce its own cultural primacy. To again quote Dr Wilson:

> I do not want to minimise the hurt felt by people involved in recent prominent instances of online abuse, or discount the extended discussion of the gendered aspects of such conflicts. But I think trolling has suddenly become a national emergency in the last week or two because it is happening to celebrities, at a time when the mass uptake of social media platforms is coinciding with a sudden acceleration in the decline of Australia's traditional media.

The notion that new freedoms for the audience somehow diminish democracy is a key aspect of elite complaints about social media. Senior British journalist Robert Fisk illustrated the point when, in a 2012 article entitled 'Anonymous Comments, Gutless Trolls, and Why It's Time We All Stop Drinking This Digital Poison', he wrote, 'Why should puerile pseudonyms be allowed to present themselves as participants in a democratic debate?'

Surely the question should be asked in reverse. In a democracy committed to notions of free speech, why shouldn't puerile pseudonyms be allowed to present themselves as participants in a democratic debate? If the best answer you have is that they are sometimes rude and upsetting, that probably isn't good enough.

The issue of civility in democratic debate is the subject of the book *Rude Democracy: civility and incivility in American politics* by US academic Susan Herbst, and in it she wrestles with the issues raised here. What I like about her take on the matter is that she in no way condones online and other forms of abuse, saying, 'There is no question … that much uncivil talk in our present-day political communication is racist, sexist, or just plain rude. No one, except a mindless provocateur, would want these sorts of hateful speech acts to be commonplace.' She argues that '[b]eing civilized, having good manners, controlling one's behavior, and showing restraint in expression are necessary (even if not sufficient) for the civility needed in a strong democratic polity', and I wouldn't disagree with that in the slightest. Such concerns were at the heart of my own struggles in moderating the comments threads at *Blogocracy*.

But Herbst also recognises that democratic debate has to be robust, perhaps even uncivil at times, and that 'it suits a democracy that [it] must wrestle with both policy and the tone of policy debate'. She makes the point that '[t]he line between passionate engagement and civility seems chronically fuzzy and arbitrary', and that although '[n]orms of civility certainly exist … civility is also very much in the eye of the beholder'. The argument about civility expressed in so many mainstream articles on trolling — typified by the *Telegraph* campaign and the comments by Paul Howes and Robert Fisk — misses the point. More accurately, debates about civility are, to quote Herbst, 'a distraction'. Civility is not a set of static rules or norms of behaviour that people veer away from because of some personal failing on their part. It is not a fixed standard against which we can judge particular individuals. It is pointless, Herbst argues, to talk in terms of now being a less civil period in our political history than some other period of time; likewise, it is unhelpful to dismiss individuals or various groups of people as civil or uncivil, as adhering to or breaking the 'rules' of civility. Given the fuzziness of the word's meaning, and the way we are likely, in political and social debate, to judge our opponents' behaviour to be uncivil while giving a pass to equivalent behaviour by those who agree with us, it is much better to see civility as a set of tools that people deploy in democratic debate in order to achieve particular ends.

In this understanding, civility — and therefore incivility — is endlessly malleable and inventive, temporary and changeable. Both are concepts deployed in order to win debates, influence people, or undermine an opponent's arguments and credibility. Ironically, or perhaps hypocritically, no one understands this strategic use of civility better than the media itself, and Herbst notes, quite rightly: 'Journalists and editors — whether they work for a television network or run an Internet site — know that incivility is just more interesting, and therefore profitable, than civility. In a society where we seek the novel, media must try harder than ever to provide it to us.'

Seen in this light, the *Telegraph*'s campaign against trolls is less to do with its stated concerns about civil discussion, and more a strategic use of civility in order to reassert the paper's primacy as a gatekeeper in the public sphere. It is an attempt to dictate the terms of engagement in an environment where the media no longer have the power to determine or control who does and who doesn't have a say. It is also in itself a commercial attempt to generate controversy in order to sell papers and maintain relevance. Paul Howes, Robert Fisk, and others who openly deplore 'attacks' on themselves and their friends via comments threads or social-media sites are being similarly calculated, asserting that their opinions are bound by standards, including the use of their own names, and that their online interlocutors are openly flouting these 'rules' and therefore are either beyond the pale of legitimate discourse or should be subject to some sort of legal sanction.

The thing that gets me about the debates over trolling is how those in relatively favoured positions when it comes to being heard in public fail to recognise that privilege, and thus seem to resent anyone getting anything like an equal say. A classic illustration of this arose in early 2013 when television host David Koch used the platform of the most successful morning program on Australian television to express the view that women should be more discreet when breastfeeding babies in public. This is a perennial hot-button topic for shows such as *Sunrise*, on which Koch is co-anchor, and so he was no doubt aware that his comments would be controversial. Indeed, he undoubtedly considers it part of his job to be controversial in this way.

Yet, as is common these days, people in Koch's position within the media often see the right to express an opinion or to be provocative as a one-way street.

So when Koch got some pushback about his views on breastfeeding, he did what many celebrities before him have done, and took to the pages of a major newspaper — *The Sydney Morning Herald* — to whinge. Under the heading 'Shocked by the Venom', he wrote:

> Why is it a crime for a bloke (and an older bloke) to have an opinion these days which isn't consistent with the noisy social media brigade? Particularly if it is regarding a subject which dares to broach family issues.
>
> The venom associated with my comments on breast-feeding has been extraordinary. From being called a buffoon with discriminatory views by the Fairfax Media critic Michael Idato, to being accused of hating kids, being jealous of babies and having a boob fetish.

Forget for a moment that if these are the worst comments he received then 'extraordinary venom' is something of an overstatement. The main point is that his argument — if you can call it that — is so lame, his shock and horror so forced, that within a couple of paragraphs he is contradicting himself. Having predicated the article on the idea that somehow people were preventing him from having an opinion, he then shifts to: 'Look, I don't have a mortgage on opinions, never have. But I have an opinion …

always have and always will. It may not be an opinion you agree with, but that is OK. It is a democracy and I am happy to hear yours.'

You can't help but wonder why, if he is so happy to hear other opinions, he wrote an article objecting to such opinions in the first place. Given this lack of coherence, it is perhaps best to see the piece as less an objection to people attacking him via email and social media and more a way of keeping the controversy alive. In other words, it is a classic example of the strategic deployment of civility in pursuit of controversy, and therefore ratings. By publishing his article, *The Sydney Morning Herald* was party to the same game.

As easy as it is to laugh off nonsense such as the David Koch article, it is still part of an overall trend wherein certain individuals — those with prestige, wealth, access to public platforms, and the ear of the powerful — seek to control public debate by attempting to define what behaviour is appropriate and what isn't. It becomes particularly egregious when the aim is specifically to invoke the law against alleged trolls, and when behaviour these powerful individuals define as bad is used to cast doubt on the validity of all forms of democratic discussion. Susan Herbst is again good on this:

> One question that arises when we treat civility and incivility
> as strategic tools is whether they are good or bad, helpful
> or hurtful for democracy. An easy answer is the one we
> so often see in the scholarly politics literature: Incivility
> is destructive and blocks proper democratic debate. I find

this a banal and unsophisticated answer, one that ignores the reality of politics, communication culture, and the social environment of the twenty-first century.

The solution is not to provide an anything-goes environment, but to recognise that many of the complaints about online incivility come from those with a vested interest in policing public speech, those whose prestige and power and income is threatened by the rise of new outlets for opinion and discussion, and who often reserve the right to engage in behaviour they find unacceptable in others. Think of the example of Alan Jones, who was attacked on social media after suggesting that then prime minister Julia Gillard's recently deceased father had 'died of shame'. Despite Jones' regular use of his radio show to stir controversy via immoderate language and abuse (behaviour deemed to have incited actual violence in the case of the so-called Cronulla race riots), he nonetheless had no qualms in turning around and accusing his social-media critics of being trolls and bullies. (Jones went so far as to call people who suggested that sponsors boycott his program 'cyber terrorists'!)

Do as I say, not as I do.

The media's hypocrisy, ignorance, and wilful blindness on these matters is one of the truly astounding revelations of the new-media age. Nothing has more exposed the fatuity of their claims to 'understand' their readers than their failure to create an environment that is truly conducive to measured democratic debate. That so many media organisations blame their readers for what they see as a breakdown in civility — to the extent of organising petitions and calling for legal sanction — is just further evidence of the divide that still exists between elements of the mainstream media and their audience.

Worse, this obsession with trolls undermines entirely media claims to be a fourth estate, a fearless bulwark against the misuses of state and private power. For while they run petitions aimed at controlling the odd outburst of disturbing behaviour by those without the power to do anything other than use bad language and make empty threats, genuine abuses of power go ignored and under-reported. Indeed, media organisations themselves pursue vendettas against their own targets, and hold sacred their right to do so. *The Australian*'s campaign against academic and independent journalist Margaret Simons is a case in point. As Robert Manne explained in his blog at *The Monthly*:

> [T]he *Australian* … devoted two front page stories, three additional stories or comments, a 'Cut and Paste' and an editorial — in total more than 6,000 words — to the Margaret Simons 'failure to disclose/conflict of interest' canard. If a Walkley Award were given to the most egregious non-story of the year, the *Australian*'s Simons saga would be a short priced favourite and a very worthy winner.
>
> The *Australian* last week attempted to damage Margaret Simons' reputation. Those who follow Australian cultural

politics closely would have been in no doubt about the motivation for the three-day-long campaign. Ordinary readers of the *Australian*, who penetrated the repetitive sludge, must however have been completely puzzled. For them, a clue lay in a couple of passing references in the 6,000 words to disagreements between Simons and the *Australian* following an August 2009 anti-terrorist police operation. The reason that Simons, who disapproved of the behaviour of the *Australian*, had been targeted was because of her outspoken and courageous criticism in this case.

The mainstream media may not descend into the bad language often associated with trolling, but their pursuit of individuals is potentially far more damaging and abusive than anything written by some random person in a comments box. Indeed, it is almost by definition worse, given the institutional and financial clout that underpins their attacks.

It should be obvious that it is unacceptable and deplorable for an anonymous commenter to take to a comments thread on a mainstream media site or their Twitter account and declare that such-and-such a celebrity should kill themselves. But surely it is many degrees of magnitude worse for a highly paid columnist to use his influence to attack individuals for not being black enough and to assert that they are using their Aboriginality to claim certain advantages, as Andrew Bolt has done. And even his behaviour pales against the systemic abuses and criminality that were uncovered in the *News of the World* scandal.

The phenomenon of trolling is related to much more important issues than anonymity or some basic moral and mental failing among our fellow citizens. Most people never get to speak, let alone be heard, in public debate. Under such circumstances, a certain amount of frustration is liable to build up, and when you combine that with a commenting facility run by journalists or media organisations who make little or no effort to police standards and who, at every point, claim for *themselves* the right to unregulated speech, is it any wonder that some people will feel entitled to give vent to their anger?

Altering this situation has nothing to do with banning anonymity or other draconian measures involving state power over free speech. Susan Herbst argues: 'Tying ourselves up in knots about what is right or wrong, civil or uncivil, is far less useful than educating Americans about how to debate and develop the thick skin that strong democratic debate demands. The real question is whether we want both depth of debate and the work that comes with it.'

That really *is* the question, for Australians as much as for Americans: do we want both the depth of debate and the work that comes with it?

This was my point in the previous chapter: engaging people in meaningful democratic debate is hard work. In the commercial environment of a mainstream-media organisation, it is time-consuming and expensive to do properly, and we should studiously ignore anyone who offers a solution that doesn't take into account the economics of doing it on the scale demanded by any site with significant community interaction.

But the mainstream media, as a key institution in a democracy, and one that prides itself on being a fourth estate — a conduit between the ordinary people and those in power — has no choice but to answer yes to Herbst's question, even understanding that it is expensive and difficult.

Unfortunately, the evidence from campaigns such as the *Telegraph's* petition to have some of their readers — the trolls — locked up for intemperate comments and bullying via social media, as well as the ongoing tendency of journalists and other elites to complain about the way their readers allegedly insult them or disagree with them, suggests that many in the mainstream are not willing to do the hard work that comes with developing the depth of debate required of an institution that claims to be the fourth estate. Instead, these media campaigns indicate a sort of divide-and-conquer mentality — any hostility detected in the readership is understood as evidence that these readers — the disagreeable ones, the argumentative ones, even the abusive ones — are somehow not really part of the audience, that they are simply troublemakers, stirrers, and malcontents whose views can marginalised by defining them as trolls.

News Limited chief executive Kim Williams illustrated the dilemma facing commercial news organisations in a speech he gave in late 2012. He began by paying homage to the openness that comes with the new technologies:

> [M]any of our journalists have moved towards a completely
> different way of interacting with their audiences. Journalists
> are no longer the gatekeepers and purveyors of unimpeachable
> wisdom. They now hold a conversation with their readers
> through the marvellous medium of digital technologies —
> changing in quite profound ways what it is that we all do.
> News.com.au is [a] strong example of what I am talking about.

The problem is that he only appears to understand the
relationship as one between a supplier and a consumer,
and his goal is to find new ways of leveraging the
changes to make money. I'm not knocking that desire;
I'm just saying that it misses the paradox at play here. By
treating their audience merely as customers, the media
are misunderstanding what has actually been unleashed
by the new technologies — namely, a redefinition of the
audience, led by the audience; people see themselves not
just as consumers but also as citizens wanting to have a
say in things that are important to them. There is no sense
that Williams understands this when he goes on to make
the point that the consumer must be 'at the centre' of what
News Limited does. The entire discussion is about people as
consumers and only as consumers:

> It's about turning our readers and viewers into valued
> customers and members of our media community. It is above
> all about getting people to subscribe to content by ensuring it
> is of the highest quality, focused on their individual interests

and delivered in a format that suits their needs. It is hardly controversial that consumers should pay for things they value and want.

Again, ultimately it is about putting consumers at the absolute centre of what we do. In ways that are commercially sustainable. So we will absolutely persist with the strategy of charging people for our journalism. We do it today with *The Australian* and the *Herald Sun*. We will next year do it with other mastheads. One of our traditional competitors recently announced it is also going to charge for digital access.

As much as people are willing to pay for content and understand that it is necessary for them to do so if that content is going to continue to exist, they do not see their relationship with news organisations as purely a commercial one. When they take to Twitter or the comments thread of an article and complain about what they are reading, they are not being a consumer in the way someone who takes back a faulty washing machine to Harvey Norman is being a consumer. They aren't just after better value for money, but a voice. They are looking for the news organisation to live up to its role as a fourth estate by treating them as citizens whose views are valued.

Let me belabour this point: there is no excusing the abuse and obscenity that is posted on social-media sites and in the comments boxes on news stories. But by constantly complaining about this minority within the audience, by going to the trouble of running campaigns against them and writing article after article alleging that people on social media are undermining democracy and that the government needs to enact new laws to keep them under control, media organisations and individual journalists are sending the message that they simply do not value their audience. People sense hostility and they end up feeling, quite justifiably, unappreciated.

How is that good business? Yes, in the short term a campaign against trolling might generate a few extra sales, but in the longer term it only serves to undermine people's trust in the media as an institution, and helps to feed the very anger that it pretends to be appalled by.

I am all for civil interaction and rules that try to ensure it, but even then, we have to accept that a certain level of incivility will exist. When such incivility does surface, it shouldn't provoke moral panic. It shouldn't be discussed as if the media were somehow neutral players in the debate, rather than businesses with a vested interest in curbing the power and influence of the various new-media organisations they are complaining about, and who themselves deploy the weapons of civility to great effect.

The mainstream media's response to trolling is an example of how, in trying to protect a status quo favourable to itself, it ends up at odds with its own audience. It leads us to the extraordinary situation where the media's most engaged readers, the ones who closely follow the news and want to participate in discussion about it, are those most likely to meet journalists' ire. This self-defeating approach is what we'll look at in the next chapter.

CHAPTER SEVEN

# *Crunching the Audience*

*I have seen grown men staring gormlessly at maps which display the demographic breakdown of their program's audience. Close to despair, they have searched for the answer to what has become for them the only question worth answering — why did the southern suburbs (or the western suburbs or the northern suburbs) turn off when we ran that story on the Middle East?*

JANA WENDT, JOURNALIST AND AUTHOR

I closed my Facebook page a few years back, during one of their ongoing adjustments to their privacy settings. I didn't use it a lot anyway, but I suddenly became creeped out by just how much personal data was leaking from my fingertips, via my keyboard, into the public sphere, and how, for all its accuracy, it could so easily be used to construct a version of me that had nothing to do with who I really was. Revelations in June 2013 that the US government, through the National Security Agency's PRISM program, has been using sites such as Facebook and Google to track the data of individuals throughout the world has simply reinforced those concerns. Yes, there are enormous advantages to having a Facebook page — or a Woolworths loyalty card, or an Amazon Wish List — but in return for the convenience, the contact with distant friends, or the knowledge that people who bought *that* book also bought *this* one, they build a world for us that is perfectly accurate and totally artificial; one in which we are no longer complex individuals but aggregations of our choices. Increasingly, we live within a statistical amphitheatre built upon data provided by everything from economic modelling to opinion poll figures to the sales information from Netflix. What's more, Big Brother is firmly ensconced in the front row of the amphitheatre, watching.

The conceit that if we know the 'facts' about people we will understand them is the foundation myth of this era of big data. Dickens' Thomas Gradgrind is its patron saint.

The technologies that have given us social media in all its forms, and that have digitised the mainstream media, have also given those who own them unprecedented powers of surveillance. Media organisations use this new surveillance technology constantly to track exactly what we are reading, which ads we click on, how long we stay on a page, and where we go once we leave a given site. No doubt some of this information is commercially useful, but the question arises: if all this data is giving the media such an accurate picture of their audience, why are so many legacy media organisations struggling to survive?

There are certain ideas about audiences that have entered deeply into the collective wisdom of the political class.

Chief among these is the idea that ordinary people are disengaged from politics. It almost doesn't matter if the assertion is true or not: if this becomes the common-sense understanding among politicians, journalists, and editors — not to mention among academics — it will affect the way politics is reported and the way these elites relate to the electorate at large.

The conclusions that journalists and editors reach about the nature of their audience have a huge impact on the way those in the media think about what they report and thus on the sort of content they provide. In other words, once you presume that the data is telling you people don't like politics, you are going to produce content that reflects that understanding, which in turn is going to affect how audiences perceive the media.

We are in the realm of the vicious circle. The political class looks at the data and plays to it, rather than realising the extent to which the audience reflected in the data is created by the choices content providers make. Academic Sally Young is excellent on this point, noting: '[T]hese audiences did not just pre-exist as some fully formed entity but were created and cultivated in particular ways by media companies.'

But let us begin by giving the data its due. The last thing I want to do here is join the ranks of those who have abandoned looking at the raw figures in favour of regurgitating the theories the voices in their guts whisper to them. We can't ignore the data, and, although there are traps in relying on an unnuanced reading of it, one of the things that lends it weight is its consistency, not just historically but also geographically. So, for instance, the data for consumption of different sorts of media in Australia shows remarkable similarities over time, as well as to that collected in the United States and Britain.

The most comprehensive recent attempt in Australia to examine what it all means is Sally Young's book *How Australia Decides: election reporting and the media.* She marshals, in magisterial fashion, data from across time and across the world and offers an authoritative discussion of its implications. She is very careful to acknowledge the controversial nature of some of the measures she relies on, and notes difficulties that arise, including the way in which people's political engagement can shift over a lifetime and how the importance of particular elections can affect that engagement in unpredictable ways. Yet despite such limitations, Young crunches the numbers and comes up with this overview:

[A]bout 5 per cent of Australians are highly interested and engaged in formal politics, while 12 per cent are so uninterested that they might not vote at all if voting were not compulsory; the other indicators suggest that up to 20 per cent are indifferent. In other words, for every Australian who is highly engaged with politics, there are at least two who aren't very interested at all. The majority of Australians are in between these two extremes.

Young distinguishes between the 'elite news audience' and the 'popular news audience', and this distinction draws upon the division of the media itself: ABC radio and television news, SBS news, broadsheet newspapers, specialist financial tabloids such as *The Australian Financial Review*, and Sunday morning politics shows such as *Insiders* are generally considered to be at the 'serious' or 'quality' end of the spectrum (though I'll note, 'quality' is a highly problematic term), while the daily tabloids, commercial talkback radio, commercial current-affairs programs, and the high-circulation women's magazines are at the other end.

Young sets out the characteristics of Australia's 'elite news audience':

> The audiences for politics-heavy news media in the 2000s differed depending on the format, but were generally dominated by men aged over 40 who were tertiary educated, well paid and in managerial or professional jobs. They were older, richer and better educated than the general population.

She goes on to say that whatever their value in terms of presenting so-called serious political coverage, the elite media did not 'have much appeal for women, the young, people who were unemployed or had low incomes or low education levels'. Additionally, blue-collar workers 'tend to prefer commercial television, tabloid newspapers and commercial radio', while younger Australians are more likely to get their news from commuter newspapers, commercial FM radio, and websites such as Google News. The data suggests, as you would expect, that 'the elite audience is vastly outnumbered by the large general audience', but also that the popular audience is 'less partisan and, in theory, more open to external influences' and 'includes more of the all-important swing voters'. As well, 'Media content tends to play an especially important role in encouraging or discouraging awareness of particular issues and in "priming" people's evaluations of parties, leaders and candidates. Media content seems to have the greatest influence on undecided voters.'

It is important to acknowledge that the categories themselves, elite and popular, are not as distinct as these descriptions make them seem. There are areas of crossover, and, as Young says, '[such information] is not meant to imply that other media consumers, such as readers of tabloid newspapers or talkback radio listeners, are not interested in politics'. Indeed, my own experience with *Blogocracy* showed just how much crossover was possible. (True, this is anecdotal, but it is based on several years of experience and tens of thousands of comments.) The blog was available through a news portal with a mass audience, and so very much on the 'popular public sphere' side of Young's division, but nonetheless it drew a dedicated and knowledgeable readership that was happy, even eager, to discuss politics. Similarly, Andrew Bolt's blog, despite existing within the tabloid world of the *Herald Sun*, discusses almost nothing but politics and is one of the masthead's biggest drawcards. Bolt is rarely accorded the credit he deserves for this, and surely there is some value to be gained from exploring how he achieves it. Critics may say he does it by appealing to the lowest-common-denominator aspect of his audience, and there is a lot of truth in that, but such thinking isn't helpful: it comes perilously close to the sort of elitist mindset that characterises ordinary people as not just disengaged but stupid, hungry for the red meat of partisan hackery and nothing more. This is precisely the sort of stereotyping I think we should avoid.

It pays to be aware, though, that the data Young and others collate is not really showing what people want in any ultimate sense, but how they choose from the options that the media make available to them. It tells us very little about what people might choose to watch, listen to, read, or share if there was other content available, or if journalists fundamentally rethought the way they present news. The data lures media producers into the belief that they are engaging with their audience and seeking to understand them, but in fact such data mining can be a very shallow sort of engagement.

Jenkins, Ford, and Green, authors of the study *Spreadable Media: creating value and meaning in a networked culture*, make a similar point in their discussion of the way that television stations use ratings figures in their attempts to define an audience:

The technologies of ratings systems attempt to render the audience visible to the television industry. Using survey technologies to achieve scale, the industry constructs a statistical representation of who might be watching and how they might be watching. This model uses demographics to segment the television audience into easily definable groups, differentiated by factors such as age, income, gender, and ethnicity, but 'the audience' is otherwise held to be relatively coherent. This approximated television audience provides the industry with a manageable object it can measure, design programming for, and sell to advertisers.

Audience members are read as 'consumers,' and ratings assume that reception (the fact that a given television set was on) equates with communication (that the message was received). This model reduces the range of factors that need to be accounted for when discussing 'watching television,' an act that occurs in a diverse array of everyday contexts and circumstances ... and with an enormous variety of audience engagement. These ratings, though a great simplification, have become the standard currency for business transactions.

This is not to say that what the ratings are measuring isn't real or accurate, only that it is selective, 'a great simplification'.

Jana Wendt, who before her retirement was the highest-paid and best-known news journalist in Australia, observed the same problem way back in 1997 when she delivered the Andrew Olle Media Lecture (one of Australian journalism's most prestigious occasions for self-reflection):

> The perversion of commercial television news and current
> affairs is due largely, I think, to the increased accuracy with
> which the viewing pulse of a select group of people around
> the country can now be monitored.
>
> A curious black box now provides TV executives with a
> minute by minute breakdown of viewing patterns every day.
>
> 'If Mrs X switched off at 6.45, there must be something
> wrong with the story we ran at 6.45', they argue, not just
> something wrong with the way they did the story, but
> something fundamentally wrong with the very subject
> matter.
>
> In other words, 'we ran a story on aboriginal children
> and some viewers switched off, now we'll think twice about
> running any other stories on aboriginal children.'
>
> This is the way many news leads not to a desire to raise
> standards or to an acceptance that not everyone will want
> to watch everything that needs to be reported, but rather to
> reluctance to run stories of a similar kind again. Never mind
> the news value, feel those ratings points.

It is a revealing observation: that the increased accuracy
of ratings measurements is leading to a fundamental
misinterpretation, or *over*-interpretation, of what the
audience wants. The significant point Wendt makes is
not that commercial television is driven by ratings per se,
but that ratings are interpreted in a particular way, one

that presumes something about the audience rather than something about the media. The idea that '[i]f Mrs X switched off at 6.45, there must be something wrong with the story ... not just something wrong with the way they did the story' is an important refocusing, and Wendt's comments challenge the assumption that audiences are disengaged, instead suggesting that the problem may be with the way news is presented.

Yet the focus on the audience that this sort of close reading of the data encourages can become compelling and take on a life of its own. Writer John Birmingham, usually a sharp observer of the media, demonstrated as much in an opinion piece in *The Sydney Morning Herald*: 'The media isn't failing because it's not giving people what they want. We know exactly what you want, even if you don't care to admit it. Worthy but dull reporting of landmark health legislation? Not so much. Upskirt shots of Lindsay Lohan spilling out of a limo at The Viper Room? Not just yes, but hell yes!'

Birmingham is not alone in these views. This sort of attitude pervades the industry, and it has come up constantly in my discussions with journalists over the past ten years or so. There is much I could say about it — most obviously, why is 'worthy but dull' reporting of policy presented as the only alternative to titillating celebrity gossip and photos? Might the presumption that all political reporting is necessarily dull, or even that 'worthy' reporting is necessarily dull, itself be part of the problem? Shouldn't the role of political journalists be to try to make worthy topics interesting? Why is a failure to engage the audience on worthy topics the audience's fault? Further, does anyone really believe that media companies — whether they be at the popular or elite end of Young's spectrum — are actually 'giving people what they want'? Surely if that were the case, they wouldn't be having so much trouble getting people to pay directly for journalism.

When such attitudes set like amalgam in the mouths of journalists and critics many reach the conclusion that people are only interested in hearing information that reinforces their pre-existing beliefs. Birmingham went on to say that '[r]eaders are naturally drawn to publications that reinforce rather than challenge their biases', an argument echoed by senior ABC journalist Mark Colvin in his 2012 Andrew Olle Media Lecture: 'You no longer need Fox News or radio shock jocks to feed your prejudices and screen out the facts. You just create a world where you get all your news from the Twitter and Facebook and blog sources you've chosen. And that world's already upon us.' Colvin presented as evidence of this a survey by the Pew research organisation in the United States, which suggests that 'a third of under thirties in the US already get their news from social media — far, far more than newspapers and equal with TV'. But this is what I mean about the difficulty involved in getting good information on people's reading and viewing habits, and then interpreting it. The view that social-media audiences are locked in an echo chamber of self-reinforcing narcissism is widely held among the political class, but that group itself might be an example of the very thing that it is trying to criticise.

Laurie Oakes, often referred to as the doyen of the Australian press gallery, its most senior and respected member, is another who shares that view. In a lecture at the 2012 Walkley Media Conference, he said:

> The emergence of politically partisan, even ideological, news outlets with their own committed audiences would be perfectly in synch with what's been happening on the Internet for some time. While it was once assumed that the Internet would help the democratic process by providing broad, diverse forums for discussions, there is concern now that it can actually narrow discussion and produce what American legal scholar Cass Sunstein calls 'group polarisation'.

Yes, there is evidence to suggest that some people prefer news that plays to their prejudices — I mean, this notion has a sort of obvious '*duh*' feel about it — but there is also evidence to suggest that that is *not* how people use social-media sites such as Facebook and Twitter.

Senior editors at ninemsn.com.au, the Australian news site with the highest traffic, are carrying out an interesting study into how people share stories online, and I must say, their work on understanding their audiences is incredibly impressive. Between March and May 2012, Andrew

Hunter and Hal Crawford collected data from 118 global news sites, looking at how their content was shared on Twitter and Facebook. In all, they looked at the 'share curve' of 1.4 million individual articles. They have only just started analysing and releasing the data via their website Share Wars, but some of their early conclusions fly in the face of the idea that people use social media as an echo chamber or as a way of exposing themselves only to content that reinforces their prejudices.

Hunter and Crawford categorise the data under three basic headings: 'norming', 'sharing', and 'newsbreaking'. For our purposes, 'norming' is the most relevant category. Crawford notes: '[W]e came to realise that a lot of what was happening with these "shared" stories was not really about sharing. Often it seemed to us to be more about reinforcing a view of the world and strengthening group identity. We called this "norming".'

On the surface, that sounds like support for the argument that social media acts as an echo chamber, but in fact Hunter and Crawford go on to note that 'norming' behaviour included sharing stories of which people both approved *and* disapproved. So while the overall aim was to reinforce group identity, it was often done by sharing stories with which people openly disagreed. In other words, they weren't just reading stories that reinforced their worldview; they were reading those that didn't. When I asked Andrew Hunter about this, he said, 'It seems some of the biggest normers are those that provoke both approval and disapproval in almost equal measures.'

I also spoke with Australian academic Mary Garden, whose doctoral research looks at this issue, and she noted an obvious flaw in some of the commentary. She told me: 'People seem to forget that Cass Sunstein only *theorised* that polarisation was occurring online. Laurie Oakes seems to have overlooked this.' Citing a 2011 study, she said, 'They found that "ideological segregation of online news consumption" was low in absolute terms; internet news consumers with homogeneous news diets are rare since not only do a significant portion of consumers get news from multiple outlets, but most online news consumption is concentrated in a small number of "large and relatively moderate sites".'

Garden also noted another survey of internet users and non-users that analysed people's news-gathering patterns in the US election season. Many users got their political information from blogs or websites, which again contradicted the 'echo chamber' theory. 'Findings suggest that internet users are more likely to expose themselves to political opinions not in agreement with their own than those who are not online,' she told me. '[The researchers] concluded that fears that getting news and information about politics online from blogs or websites might "channel people into informational warrens of one-sided arguments" are not borne out by their data.

'They acknowledge that one of the major concerns about people's use of the internet is one which Sunstein cautions about: that the powerful filtering mechanisms available online means people can avoid information that does not support their beliefs. However, a second survey conducted five months later provided further support that blog readers are more likely to encounter contrary information and political views which do not accord with their beliefs, and "selective exposure" did not appear to be a typical pattern of internet users.

'They found that 31 per cent of internet users preferred neutral sources for political information; the remainder were divided evenly between preferences for sites that agreed with their political views and sites that challenged their political views.'

Just as some media organisations accuse unwanted commenters and critics of being rude, disrespectful, unprofessional, and abusive — of being trolls — while encouraging those very qualities in some of their most successful and high-profile columnists and on-air 'personalities', so some sections of the media use the insult 'echo chamber' to describe social media, even though they themselves fit the definition of such an ingrown environment. The press gallery — a small, self-contained group of journalists who work in close contact with the politicians, staffers, and bureaucrats they write about — could legitimately be criticised as an echo chamber, but the description also fits particular news outlets. *The Australian*, for instance, in an October 2012 editorial, saw fit to say (with withering contempt), 'The twitterati are, of course, entitled to their views but the government's problem is that it dips into this leftist, activist echo chamber and seeks its validation, encouraging itself down a futile path.' Of course, the editorialists are entitled to their views too, but accusing Twitter of being any sort of echo chamber is a pretty funny insult for a right-of-centre newspaper with — according to figures released by the Audit Bureau of Circulations in February 2013 — a circulation of around 124,000 (down 8.4 per cent on weekdays and down 9.6 per cent on weekends over the previous quarter) to hurl. Especially when figures from April 2013, collated by *SocialMediaNews,* show Twitter's Australian users number an estimated 2.1 million, while those using Facebook come in at an astonishing 11.5 million. Just who is preaching to the converted here?

So the idea of the echo chamber starts to look like another concept, like trolling, that many in the media use as a bulwark against criticism. It is less a meaningful concept and more a conveniently blurry claim to wield against the growing number of critics (audience members) who use social media to express their dissatisfaction with the media products on offer. And like the use of the word 'trolls', its deployment exhibits an element of projection.

Again, the point is not to ignore the data but to try to understand it in a more nuanced way; to not over-interpret it. One of the most interesting observations Sally Young makes about the manner in which audiences consume news is this:

While most Australians are not particularly interested in politics, they are interested in news ... By 2008, over 80 per cent were still reporting that they would catch up with the news during their day ... Even at the end of the 2000s, news and current affairs programs continued to top television ratings in Australia, which was unusual by international standards ... General news, sport, entertainment and music were the types of news Australians said they preferred, with 'political analysis' ranked last.

Now, one obvious way to understand this is to conclude that Australians are disengaged from politics. But a better conclusion might be that they are disengaged from the way that politics is conducted, both by politicians and by the media. At the very least, such data raises again the question of how we separate the way politics is practised from the way it is reported. If, as Young and many others suggest, the data shows that most people get their political information from the mainstream media, especially television, it is reasonable to conclude that the lack of interest in political news has at least something to do with the way it is presented by the media. Young makes this point herself when she notes that

there was an odd paradox at work in the 2000s: respondents said they were more interested in politics, but fewer were following it closely through the media. Is this because people *were* interested in traditional politics but found its actual conduct disappointing? Or was it because people were dissatisfied with the way the media reported politics?

Young doesn't answer the question outright, but it is hard to see how media coverage could be anything other than crucial in determining people's level of interest in the media coverage of politics. In other words, you can't conclude that people aren't interested in politics just because they aren't interested in following it in the media. And you don't have to think very hard to see that a vicious circle is set up, where inadequate coverage of politics leads politicians to behave in a particular way, which leads to the media behaving in a particular way, which leads to a sort of generalised despair among the audience and a diminished interest in politics and the media's coverage of it. This view was at the heart of Lindsay Tanner's book *Sideshow: dumbing down democracy*:

> Under siege from commercial pressures and technological innovation, the media are retreating into an entertainment frame that has little tolerance for [complexity]. In turn, politicians and parties are adapting their behaviour to suit the new rules of the game ... While its outward forms remain in place, the quality of our democracy is being undermined from within ...
>
> The sideshow syndrome is eroding public faith in democratic politics. As political coverage gets sillier, politicians are forced to get sillier to get coverage. The antics,

hyperbole, and spin that have eventuated now alienate many voters.

Judith Brett is another academic who has looked at people's engagement with politics, but she has taken a different approach. Using a series of interviews with 75 people in the years 1986–1990 and 2002–2004, Brett and colleague Anthony Moran offer a less quantitative view of public engagement with politics. In so doing, they note some problems with the number-driven approach itself, saying, 'Since World War Two the detailed social knowledge and intuitive hunches which once guided politicians' and journalists' judgements about what the public thought and felt have been replaced by increasingly sophisticated techniques of opinion polling.' Brett continues:

> Such research not only maps people's opinions; it also regularly checks their demographic and socio-economic characteristics, providing policy-makers with statistical maps of the country, as policy making becomes ever more expert and technocratic. For, despite the democratic impulse behind public opinion polling's attention to what people think, the techniques drain agency from people. Citizens as active members of the body politic become customers of government service delivery … and in the private talk of politicians and their factotums they are often referred to simply as 'the mob'.

This ongoing polling is a type of surveillance. It is as much an attempt to control as it is to understand, and by creating bloodless, statistical caricatures of 'ordinary people', it forces — let's say encourages — responses that may not be appropriate, let alone complete. It leads to stereotyping and to the exclusion of other possible ways of reporting and engaging with the audience. Writing in *The Australian Financial Review,* Mark Latham made this point during the 2013 election campaign, when then prime minister Julia Gillard announced that she was to spend a week campaigning in the marginal and critical seats of western Sydney:

> On Tuesday afternoon, when the Sky News guru David Speers spoke about the Prime Minister's impending visit to western Sydney, including the novelty of an overnight stay, the station screened footage of dilapidated public housing stock.
>
> The inference was clear: this was the type of accommodation Julia Gillard would have to choose from when bunking down out west.
>
> It was a small but instructive example of the media's stereotyping of the region.

Latham provided data that showed western Sydney is in fact culturally diverse, with a growing percentage of professional workers who are gradually displacing the traditional blue-collar base. He lamented the ill-informed framing used by the media, saying, 'In most political commentaries [western Sydney is] treated as an oddity, a strange destination at the end of Sydney's motorways, an outpost to which journalists venture only when their work requires it. Already in the analysis of this year's federal election we have become the bearded lady along the sideshow alley of Australian politics.'

When you see media coverage like this, which not only misrepresents political and social reality but also proceeds to offer analysis and conclusions based upon that misrepresentation, you really have to wonder about the accusation that ordinary people are disengaged from politics. I mean, who is actually disengaged here? What is this sort of reporting reflecting other than a fundamental disconnect between journalists and their audience? It harks back precisely to the point Margo Kingston made in her book about Pauline Hanson's 1998 election campaign — that journalists had entered into a compact with politicians to present political reality in a particular way: 'We pick their spin, they pick ours, and both sides look only at each other, as journalists present our theatre reviews to an ever more disconnected public.'

The question is whether the advent of new media, of the whole panoply of websites, blogs, social-media outlets, and the like, has changed the basic profile of audience participation in, and discussion of, politics, and whether it does, as so many claim, challenge the view of the audience as disengaged. Again, let's turn to the data and see what it offers.

Despite the huge amount of proselytising done on behalf of new media as a saviour of democracy, a rebirth of grassroots participation, and an alternative source of information about politics and important social and cultural issues, the evidence — the hard data — is less than encouraging. The usual caveats apply, but the trend that seems to have emerged throughout the 2000s is that new media is replicating the structures and practices of the old media, rather than growing a new audience for political discussion. New media has simply shifted a certain segment of the elite audience from traditional sources of information — especially the broadsheet newspapers — to blogs and other websites.

To my mind, one of the most tiresome debates about democracy and new versus old media is that between the so-called cyber enthusiasts and cyber sceptics. Both sides engage in a straw-man extravaganza of claim and counterclaim about the influence, reach, relevance, and resilience of online media, and the alleged concomitant decline and fall of more traditional sources. The argument is fed by the fact that hard data on internet usage has been patchy and unreliable, leaving plenty of space for gut feelings and cheer-squadding to rear their opportunistic heads. Still, the only thing more yawn-worthy than taking sides would be to try to assume some sort of superior, balanced middle view, sweetly claiming that both sides have valid points to make. So I won't.

Let's note, then, that there is no denying the revolutionary impact of the new technologies. They have fundamentally changed the game in terms of the economics of news reporting and the relationship between the media and its audience. So it is worth looking at what we can glean from the data for online readerships and what it might say about the future of that central relationship.

Sally Young concludes that 'there was no indication the internet has attracted a different audience from that which sought traditional elite news'. It is the elite audience — the older, predominantly male, better educated, higher-income person — that is using the internet to access news, and these people have not appeared out of nowhere but have shifted their reading and viewing habits from other, more traditional forms of elite media, especially the broadsheet newspapers. The online audience is broader in that it tends to be younger and slightly wealthier than that for traditional media, but as Young says, it 'is still firmly within the realms of the elite'.

Research by American academic Matthew Hindman, published in his 2009 book *The Myth of Digital Democracy*, bears out the thrust of Young's discussion, and expands on it in interesting and important ways. Central to Hindman's argument is the claim that 'the Internet is not eliminating exclusivity in political life; instead, it is shifting the bar of exclusivity from the production to the filtering of political information'. In other words, almost anyone can now be a content producer, but only a very few are ever read, let alone heard. Hindman cites several aspects of the architecture of the online environment

— the software that allows it to operate, the network protocols that allow computers to talk to each other — as evidence of how this filtering is happening, and why it is increasing rather than eliminating the sort of exclusivity that hampers traditional media. Key among these factors are the links that allow users to navigate between sites, and the way that search engines, particularly Google, assign value to these links:

> [T]he most important filtering … is not conscious at all; it is rather a product of the larger ecology of online information. The link structure of the Web is critical in determining what content citizens see. Links are one way that users travel from one site to another; all else being equal, the more paths there are to a site, the more traffic it will receive. The pattern of links that lead to a site also largely determines its rank in search engine results.

Hindman provides solid evidence that this underlying structure leads to a concentration of content in what he calls 'winner-take-all' patterns, which is to say that 'communities of Web sites on different political topics are each dominated by a small set of highly successful sites'. This concentration is so intense that, in Hindman's view, any claim that the internet is leading to a democratisation of political discussion and engagement is ridiculous — quite a bitter pill for even the mildest cyber enthusiasts to swallow. And it gets even worse; he continues, 'Who speaks and who gets heard [are] two separate questions. On the Internet, the link between the two is weaker than it is in almost any other area of political life.'

So the ease with which individuals can post comments online is almost counterproductive, and it is certainly only, as Hindman puts it, 'openness in the most trivial sense'. Your online visibility — your ability to be heard — is influenced first and foremost by who links to you, which in turn determines how search engines rank you, and the indisputable fact is that this architecture of links and search-engine rank enormously favours a handful of elite sites. What's more, the way people use search engines is 'shallow'; people tend to use them to find site-specific locations rather than particular content, and this limits the number of sites a person is exposed to, especially if they only click on the first couple of search results that come up. Hindman says, 'the search strategies that citizens employ limit the political content they see'.

We therefore need to modify the conclusions that Young left us with. She stated that the web has not attracted a new cohort of users but rather cannibalised users from traditional, elite sources of information such as broadsheets. Hindman's research suggests that what has in fact happened is a kind of bipolar split. He says that '[i]n nearly every online niche', what arises is 'a small set of winners that receive the lion's share of the traffic, and a host of tiny Web sites that, collectively, receive most of the remaining visitors'. Hindman calls this phenomenon 'the missing middle' and suggests that it helps to explain 'many puzzling contradictions in Internet politics'.

Speaking specifically of blogs, Hindman shows that while 'blogs may reach only a fraction of the public', they are now 'the most widely read form of U.S. political commentary'. This appears to fit nicely with the idea of online commentary and independent journalism being some sort of liberating force or viable alternative to the traditional mainstream, but the situation is more complex. 'While the tail of the distribution includes many hundreds of thousands of political bloggers,' Hindman says, 'a small group of A-list bloggers actually gets more political blog traffic than the rest of the citizenry combined.'

Let that fact sink in for a moment. The usual complaint about news moving online is that it leads to a massive fragmentation of topics and audiences, but Hindman's work suggests the opposite — a level of concentration in the top ten to 20 online sites that is actually greater than that which occurs in traditional media.

As brilliant as a lot of Hindman's analysis is, I don't agree with everything he says. His attempt to show that the major US bloggers are in fact 'more elite' than the elite columnists of the mainstream, for example, is overstated. He looks at the class background of the main writers at the most trafficked-to blogs in the United States and notes that they tend to be older, male, and white, with 60 per cent of them having either degrees or experience in journalism. Sure, they fit the profile, but I wonder if you can just leave it at that? Even if we are talking about a demographic that conforms to a particular profile, these writers were still relative nobodies within it but were nonetheless able to attract an audience at the expense of their more experienced and much better financed peers in the mainstream. They might in one sense be reinforcing the structures of the traditional media, by being demographically similar to the mainstream's leading columnists, but they rewrote the rulebook on how to engage with their audiences. This in itself is an incredible structural change, even if the underlying architecture of the web mitigates against the full value of that change being realised.

Nonetheless, Hindman presents powerful evidence for his contentions about the way the structure of the web governs our usage of it, and he is aware of the fact that the web can't be viewed in isolation from other centres of power and influence. And I must admit, not only are the criticisms I have read of his work less than convincing, but also his analysis rings true simply because it mirrors so much of my own experience as both a content producer and as a media consumer.

So where does all this leave us? Central to a lot of cyber enthusiasm is the presumption that a better-informed electorate makes for a better functioning democracy. Thus, the argument goes, by allowing people to better access information online, we are gradually getting just that, a better-informed electorate. But the evidence is problematic. A strong explanation for this is that, despite the potentially revolutionary nature of new technologies, they are still embedded in a web architecture and pre-existing societal structures that are resistant to change. Sally Young says, 'we have to recognise that existing social, political and economic structures have an impact on how the new technology is used', and that so far 'much of the evidence suggests the internet has been "normalised into the traditional political world" with existing inequities continued online'. The bottom line is that, for most of what Young calls the popular audience, the rise and rise of new media and social media probably hasn't made a whole lot of difference to their engagement with politics and their sense of themselves within the democratic fabric of society. To which I would add that the failure to use these wonderful new communication tools to engage the *popular* audience is a failure not just of the political class, not just of the traditional media companies, but also of new-media practitioners, and I include myself in that. But none of this is an excuse for falling into the vicious circle that I've described above. As Judith Brett says, 'Political elites regularly bemoan the political apathy of ordinary people, seeing their poor knowledge and limited interest as a failure or lack, rather than as a reasoned response to experience. Predictably, they call for more civic education in school, rather than for institutional reforms that would give people more reason to engage.'

It really is the height of hypocrisy, not to mention laziness, for the media to presume that people aren't interested in politics because they seem less than enthralled by the way the media covers it. Unfortunately, as the new commercial environment increases the pressure to generate profits and therefore the pressure on journalists themselves, it becomes even more tempting for journalists and editors to fall back on these excuses, and to assert that people aren't really interested.

No one should play down the disruptive influence of the new technologies, but the basic issue — problems with how political journalists do their job — well and truly predates the rise of online media. Academic Julianne Schultz, writing back in 1998, noted in her book *Reviving the Fourth Estate: democracy, accountability and the media* that even then commercial pressures were leading media organisations to ignore more serious, investigative stories:

> The capacity for the ideal of the Fourth Estate to continue to be relevant to the practice of Australian journalism will depend on the continued vigilance and insistence of journalists and editors, their willingness to accept a greater degree of accountability and attempts to understand public opinion ...
>
> If journalists were able to build more meaningful, reflective alliances with their audiences, they could become a more significant democratic force.

My argument is that such alliances could make them a more successful commercial force, too.

Jenkins, Ford, and Green make a point in their discussion of soap-opera audiences (and there is certainly an element of soap opera about media coverage of politics) that is relevant here. They write that '[f]ans and other active audiences develop an expertise in the content and a mastery of distribution technologies which increase their stakes in these media properties', and that '[w]hile many people in the soap opera industry bemoan fans' constant complaining, the fan parodies and rants that result may encourage viewers to hold onto the community they have built around the ritual of watching the program'. It's blindingly obvious, really. The most engaged members of the audience are likely to be the most critical. And journalists and media organisations attack the most engaged part of the audience to reassert their disappearing power as gatekeepers.

I don't think we can get away from the fact that the best data we have indicates that only a relatively small percentage of citizens — maybe 12 per cent — regularly engage with politics as it is presented in the mainstream media. This is a collective failure by more than just the media. But the problem is that journalists and editors and producers use this fact to assume a more general disengagement from politics and craft their coverage and content accordingly, presuming that all the blame lies with the audience. Under such circumstances, disengagement becomes a self-fulfilling prophecy.

And here's a final point. Even if only a relatively small percentage of people are deeply engaged with political reporting, the rest of the audience, I suspect, uses political coverage as a guide to the integrity and trustworthiness of the media as a whole. The disappearance of more serious content in favour of the celebrity gossip and other titillating information that click-throughs apparently show we want is actually undermining the appeal of various news outlets, even among those who appear not to be accessing political journalism.

Journalists often argue that politicians risk alienating the electorate by relying too heavily on opinion polls and that, despite their stated preferences, voters sometimes want a government to take a stand — to do what they think is right, rather than popular — and I'm quite sure that analysis is correct. It is strange, then, that media organisations don't apply the same logic to their own product: maybe, rather than pandering to what the data allegedly shows are people's stated preferences, they should make a commitment to solid political journalism that treats the audience as valued citizens. Julianne Schultz calls this sort of approach a 'revival of professionalism' and says it

> will require a new willingness to engage in reflective analysis of journalistic methods and aims, and an attempt to build new alliances with the media-consuming public … If reporters, editors and producers are able to reach out to their public as citizens — rather than merely as consumers, victims or talent — alliances may be able to be built.

I go back to Sally Young's point that audiences were created and cultivated in particular ways by media companies. The media are not just selling widgets; they are in a market that deals in far less quantifiable matters, such as social and political values. Kate Crawford, a principal researcher at Microsoft Research, is blunt about the risks of relying on quantitative data in such situations. In an article in *The Wall Street Journal*, she writes:

> Data and data sets are not objective; they are creations of human design. We give numbers their voice, draw inferences from them, and define their meaning through our interpretations. Hidden biases in both the collection and analysis stages present considerable risks, and are as important to the big-data equation as the numbers themselves.

Or as writer and researcher Evgeny Morozov says in his book *To Save Everything, Click Here: the folly of technological solutionism*, 'Quantifiable information might be nothing but low-hanging fruit that is easy to pick but often thwarts more ambitious, more sustained efforts at understanding.'

That more ambitious and sustained understanding can only be reached through a comprehensive and less confrontational engagement with audiences. Audience figures show that there is a vast middle section — the majority between the elite and popular audiences — that could be enticed to follow political issues more closely if the media presented those stories differently. But before journalists and editors can hope to reach that sector of the public and win back their trust and their interest, they are going to have to connect with the highly engaged section who are currently the media's most severe critics.

When you see an industry in as much commercial trouble as the media, you have to conclude that they are doing something wrong. Unfortunately, most analysis begins and ends with a bland statement that the media's business model has been undermined by online technologies and that they need a replacement source of revenue, and that once they find it, everything will be all right. Forget for a moment that no such magic bullet is likely to exist; the real problem with this sort of thinking is that it misses the crucial point: that the traditional business model was predicated on a massive disconnect between the journalism and the people consuming it. Because the consumers of news weren't directly paying for what they were reading and watching and listening to, that disconnect created a distance between the media and their audience. It is not just the business model that is broken, but the relationship between the media and their audience.

Data is not destiny. If traditional media organisations are going to thrive, they are going to have to nurture new audiences into existence. They are going to have to gather *knowledge* of we the people, not just mine information about us. In an era where audiences are more and more often being asked to pay directly for their news, dismissing them as 'disengaged', as if it were entirely their fault, as if it were an immutable truth, is simply no longer an option.

## CHAPTER EIGHT

# The New Front Page

*Every journalist who is not too stupid or too full of himself to notice
what is going on knows that what he does is morally indefensible.
He is a kind of confidence man, preying on people's vanity,
ignorance, or loneliness, gaining their trust and betraying them
without remorse ... Journalists justify their treachery in various
ways according to their temperaments. The more pompous talk about
freedom of speech and 'the public's right to know'; the least talented
talk about Art; the seemliest murmur about earning a living.*

JANET MALCOLM, JOURNALIST AND AUTHOR

Towards the end of 2012 I wrote a piece for *The Drum*
in which I suggested that bloggers and other freelance
writers needed a professional association, a body that
could gain standing in the community so that its members
could be accorded some of the benefits of access enjoyed
by mainstream journalists. The piece came about after
a talk with Julian Disney, the chair of the Australian
Press Council. 'The idea,' I wrote, 'is not to create a body
of people doing the same work as regular journalists, but
to encourage alternative views into the public sphere by
closing the clout gap currently experienced by bloggers and
other online writers.'

In May 2013, the Media Entertainment and Arts Alliance, the union that represents workers across the media and entertainment industries in Australia, launched a new membership category called Freelance Pro, which provides the sorts of benefits my *Drum* article had suggested, including professional liability insurance, help with contract negotiations, and a card that gives members access to press conferences and other events generally reserved for journalists. I was pleased to be one of those asked to speak at the Melbourne launch of the project.

Freelance Pro is a measure of how far blogging and other amateur forays into journalism-related activities have come since the days of *Surfdom*; such a development was unimaginable back then. But I don't think it should kick off any triumphalism or backslapping of the kind that we have seen at different moments in the past as social media has developed. Too much is still uncertain.

As critical as I have been of the mainstream media throughout this book, it is not my intention to suggest that the way forward is simply to replace that mainstream with a hearty band of bloggers and citizen journalists. The idea that a dedicated and knowledgeable individual or a small group of writers can somehow replicate and improve upon the expensive, intrusive, and confrontational work of the newsrooms of the mainstream media on a sustained basis is, to my way of thinking, a fantasy. It may be possible in certain instances, and there are any number of examples of excellent journalism by individuals either working alone or attached to small outfits such as *New Matilda* and *Crikey* (though even then, we are largely talking about professional journalists such as Ben Eltham, rather than new-media amateurs). But the ongoing, tedious, and time-consuming work that is beat journalism — and that is fundamental to our democracy — can only be carried out by a mainstream media big enough to pay for it and powerful enough to stand up to intimidation from the power centres it investigates. Critics on social media and elsewhere are quite correct to point out how badly the mainstream often does this work, and all power to them. But no matter how righteous such complaints are, the fact is — and let me put this bluntly — democracies need a mainstream media more than they need citizen journalists.

The point is well made by writer and former journalist David Simon, the man who created two of the greatest television series of all time, *The Wire* and *Treme*. In testimony before a Senate committee in the United States, Simon said:

> [H]igh-end journalism — that which acquires essential information about our government and society in the first place — is a profession; it requires daily, full-time commitment by trained men and women who return to the same beats day in and day out until the best of them know everything with which a given institution is contending. For a relatively brief period in American history — no more

than the last fifty years or so — a lot of smart and talented people were paid a living wage and benefits to challenge the unrestrained authority of our institutions and to hold those institutions to task. Modern newspaper reporting was the hardest and in some ways most gratifying job I ever had. I am offended to think that anyone, anywhere believes American institutions as insulated, self-preserving and self-justifying as police departments, school systems, legislatures and chief executives can be held to gathered facts by amateurs pursuing the task without compensation, training or, for that matter, sufficient standing to make public officials even care to whom it is they are lying or from whom they are withholding information.

Like a lot of people, I am more than happy to pay for journalism (and in fact I do, via various subscriptions, paywalls, and contributions to independent journalists), but I won't pay for rubbish. This doesn't mean I'm only interested in highfalutin, long, well-researched pieces on political policy, and detailed backgrounders on everything from the financial crisis in Europe to the life and times of Eddie Obeid. I'll take my fair share of junk, too. Like many, I'm happy to see a bit of celebrity gossip or the odd man-bites-dog story in my daily mix, and will admit I'm just as likely to click on the video of the cat feeding a bottle of milk to the marmoset as the next person. But a willingness to accept such ephemera does not mean that I don't also want serious journalism. You can't count my clicks on the rubbish stories and presume that I only want more of them. I also need coverage of politics and other matters of social importance that affect my understanding of the world, and that will inform me as a citizen and not just as a consumer. I need to be able to trust those stories and I need them presented in a way that is transparent, in a way that shows journalists understand that they are not just messengers but also shapers of news.

Yet we've seen by now that the media often has trouble meeting this minimal standard, and the interesting thing to me, as someone who regularly writes articles criticising the media, is that journalists know this better than anyone. It astounds me how often, after such pieces appear, journalists contact me privately to tell me that they agree with the criticism. They won't endorse my views in public, but they want me to know they agree. I'm not quite sure where this reticence comes from, but I suspect it is a sort of professional solidarity: there are enough people out there already tipping a bucket on the industry without them joining in. Of course, there is an element of self-preservation, too. In a small market such as Australia, no journalist wants to criticise a given company too ferociously: you never know when you are going to need a job from them — especially in a period where full-time jobs in journalism are disappearing like chalk marks in a storm.

Still, you don't have to dig too hard to find examples of journalists voicing their concerns publicly. A recent survey conducted by the Walkley Foundation and several Australian universities reported some astonishing results. They interviewed 100 newspaper journalists, including editors, deputy editors, chiefs of staff, and senior journalists — the very people who are guiding their companies' responses to the changed media environment. Only 38 per cent of them thought the quality of Australian newspaper journalism was 'excellent'. Thirty-four per cent said it was 'average', while 28 per cent rated it 'poor'. That's a total of 62 per cent who thought newspapers were producing material that was average or poor. These aren't trolls out there in social-media land letting off steam; they are key figures in the industry. It's an extraordinary vote of diminished confidence.

At a conference in early 2013, senior political writer with *The Australian Financial Review* Laura Tingle was asked about problems in the industry. She said:

> The change in the economics of the media and the change in the way the media works means that we no longer have specialists in [various] areas anymore. Now that sounds like a really small thing, but it means that when a story is reported, it's reported by generalist reporters.
>
> In Canberra we're political reporters and we tend to report it ... as a political story, as a matter of political controversy. There aren't the people in the key offices of the newspapers who would have written really detailed, well-informed pieces backgrounding these issues ... There aren't

people there who've got their own interest in getting those stories into the paper. It's as brutal and basic as that.

Here's another brutal and basic fact: if you had relied on the mainstream media for information on important world issues such as the Iraq War, climate change, the events leading up to the global financial crisis, and even media reform — especially if you were part of the vast middle, that part of the audience that only dips in and out of such issues — you would have been badly informed. This was true not just in Australia. On all of these issues, the mainstream failed in its most basic duty as a provider of information that allows citizens to inform themselves. It found itself captured by various special interests, including the most special one of all: self-interest. The Bush administration and its 'coalition of the willing' convinced allegedly hardened, sceptical journalists that Saddam Hussein had weapons of mass destruction and thus used them to help justify a war. Various industry-funded think tanks and individuals have managed to insert themselves into the discussion on climate change as a legitimate alternative view, despite their 'arguments' being contradicted by the vast majority of experts in the field. The huge apparatus of alleged experts reporting on finance and other matters to do with the economy failed to note the market manipulation occurring prior to 2008 that precipitated the global financial meltdown. The coverage of the case for changes to media regulation has been farcical, with media organisations using their position to argue an incredibly self-serving response to the government's proposals. In the words of British writer and editor Dan Hind, 'Public communication has broken down to the point where we lack the means to establish an accurate account of the world as the basis for common deliberation.'

But it isn't just the big stories that point to a fundamental problem with the role of the media in public discussion. Something essential is broken in the industry's most basic understanding of how it does its job, and it has nothing to do with diminishing profits or the rise of social media. The matter was perfectly illustrated by a recent post at Australian blog *Club Troppo* written by economist Richard T. Green. He cites what he calls an unimportant and innocuous story about the fishing industry in South Australia:

It is headlined (on the website) and introduced thus.

> **Australia's seafood capital under pressure from imports**
> *TONY EASTLEY: Port Lincoln calls itself Australia's seafood capital. On South Australia's Eyre Peninsula, it's home to the nation's largest commercial fishing fleet.*
>
> *It's a major exporter of both wild and aquaculture products, but it's coming under increasing pressure from imports.*
>
> *For instance, it's reported that around half of the barramundi consumed in Australia comes from Asia.*

*Barramundi is known by many around the world as Asian sea bass, although its scientific common name is barramundi perch.*

Then the actual story begins.

*TIM JEANES: Sitting by a boat ramp next to the city's maritime museum, one of Port Lincoln's pioneer tuna fishermen Hagen Stehr looks out to the waters of Spencer Gulf and sees good times ahead thanks to China.*

You might notice that contra to the introduction, Mr Stehr seems neither 'under pressure', nor concerned about imports. In fact, he seems very positive about the future of his industry. You may even notice that Port Lincoln's Barramundi industry is much more impaired by the difficulties a tropical fish faces in the Southern Ocean than the spectre of imports.

In fact, the entire premise of the introduction is not supported, and indeed is only tangentially related to the actual report ... I don't get why our media does this. I don't know why casual dishonesty leaks through every aspect of what they do.

My guess is that it has to do with a culture, a professional practice, that has never had to answer to any authority outside itself, has traditionally faced little competition, and has thus become lazy and blind to its own faults. It has to do with an industry that has never really had to deal with its audience and be responsible to it in the way that Green, via his access to social media, is demanding. The net effect, as Green notes, is that 'people tune out ... It loses them respect, it poisons debate, and it is sending them bankrupt'.

The story in question is hardly a matter of international or even national importance, but that is exactly the point. 'It is the sheer lack of reasons to distort the story,' Green writes, 'that makes it so disturbing. It's dishonesty in service of no-one ... It's just how things are done.' And then he puts bluntly a point I've been making throughout this book: 'If we can't trust them to cut back on the bullshit on even the most unimportant, innocuous topics, how can we ever hope to trust them on anything that really matters?'

Green is talking about something more fundamental than simply getting facts wrong. He is talking about a systematic distortion in the way information is presented that seems to be built into the media's modus operandi. Concern about this stuff mightn't show up in the endless quantitative audience surveys media companies carry out, but media professionals are kidding themselves if they think that a significant section of the audience doesn't notice.

Yet on the more basic level we should also have concerns about errors of fact. I am amazed at how blind media organisations are to the idea that trying to hide their mistakes or pretend they don't exist completely undermines audience trust in the rest of their work. The problem isn't that mainstream media organisations get things wrong; it is that they so often refuse to admit it and make corrections. What's more, such companies act as if social media had never been invented, and try to tough out criticisms, or ignore them in the hope they will go away. When a storm on Twitter or Facebook makes that impossible, the tendency is too often to attack the critics — to, ironically, shoot the messenger — rather than concede the original mistake.

Often it doesn't take a storm for journalists to hit out. Twitter is a hotbed of fractious exchanges between media and audience, and the heat they generate is often in inverse proportion to the seriousness of the topic.

One telling example is the exchange between Marcus Priest of *The Australian Financial Review* and Greg Jericho, a blogger and author whose thoughts on economics have made him a favourite on *The Drum* and have garnered him a large following on social media.

In March 2013 Jericho (known on Twitter as @GrogsGamut) commented in passing that he wished the *AFR* offered some sort of price differential on its online subscription prices, saying he 'would pay a reduced sub for just the politics in the AFR and not the company/business news'. His interlocutor, who uses the Twitter screen name of @Drag0nista, responded, 'I reckon they should have a pay per view, like they used to in the old days', and in turn Jericho said, 'or at least bundled packages like Foxtel has — go premium or chose [*sic*] not to be able to see certain sections'.

Then Marcus Priest, an *AFR* journalist, intervened: 'What is this conversation thread? AFR Cheapskates Anonymous?' Jericho responded to what I imagine he thought was a playful jibe by saying, 'no it's the "Don't want to pay for stuff I don't read Anonymous"'.

But any sense that Priest was being playful evaporated as the conversation continued. He became condescending: 'Good journalism like @latingle @PhillipCoorey needs people to buy subscriptions or you'll end up with the very thing you complain about — bad journalism'. Talk about miss the point.

Jericho responded, 'I'm not interested in paying $59 a month just to read Laura Tingle', while Drag0nista added, 'I think @GrogsGamut's point is that he would pay to read @latingle @PhillipCoorey, but not the full $59/month'.

Priest, instead of engaging with what is a reasonable discussion about how best to price online access, decided to lay down the law: 'My point is you can't pick and choose'.

Well, actually, that was Jericho's point, and he, as a consumer, was expressing the view that he would be more likely to buy a subscription if the *AFR* were more flexible in its pricing; that is, if he *could* pick and choose. He wasn't being cheap; he was being discerning, as is his right as a customer. It was a distinction lost on Marcus Priest.

Jericho got a bit snarky and said, 'and how's that business model working out for you?', which was all the provocation Priest needed: 'not well when there are cheapskates like you who want something for nothing'.

Seriously?

Clearly, Jericho had never said he wanted free access, so he restated his point: 'I don't want something for nothing. I just don't want to pay for things I don't want!'

Priest then descended into the sort of behaviour that would be considered unacceptable in a teenager working part-time at a corner store. He started insulting his customer.

Priest (@MeddlesomPriest): Sounds suspiciously like an argument for not paying tax

Jericho (@GrogsGamut): so you're saying the AFR is now a public institution that I can vote on who edits it, and what it covers?

Priest (@MeddlesomPriest): Er no. Don't be a dill. What I'm saying is there are lots of things we have to pay for which we want only bit of but not all of.

Jericho (@GrogsGamut): ok — give me some examples in your daily life.

Priest (@MeddlesomPriest): och aye you remind me of my mate who complains the beer is too expensive and spends the night drinking from others glasses.

Jericho (@GrogsGamut): really? You think Foxtel is stupid for offering different subscription packages? That's all I'm suggesting. That you think offering different levels of subscription is radical is truly astonishing. But please keep attacking me personally, if you think that helps your case.

Priest (@MeddlesomPriest): I'll take a big guess and bet that even if such a thing existed you would still complain about the price. you're pretty thin skinned if you think I am attacking you personally

Jericho (@GrogsGamut): you called me a cheapskate. Have I called you anything at all?

Priest (@MeddlesomPriest): oh dear. So sorry

Incredibly, another *AFR* journalist, Phil Coorey, butted in and continued the attack upon Jericho. He tweeted: 'sadly, we can't all be blogging on the taxpayer's dime'. This was an ill-directed reference to Jericho's former job in the public service: at the time News Limited had accused him of blogging when he was at work. The charge was scurrilous and had been revealed as such. To allude to it now, when Jericho no longer worked for the public service, was irrelevant and borderline dishonest.

It is an astounding encounter. Here we have two senior journalists attacking a customer in public for daring to express a preference about how the company that employs them prices its product. Jericho now also writes for the Australian edition of *The Guardian*, so he is not your standard customer, but he is followed by many who are, and they, too, would have seen the exchange. Yes, the matter is ultimately quite petty, but that's the point. Why would two senior journalists think that it was in any way wise or acceptable to engage in this sort of exchange in front of the people they are relying on to buy their product? It is a vivid illustration not just of how divorced some journalists are from their audiences, but also of how they fail to realise that they are now the retail face of their industry. In a world where your work is paid for indirectly via advertising, it is easy to see how such a distance (and such contempt) might develop. In a world where you actually need individuals to cough up cash directly for the work you are selling, however, it is a form of professional suicide.

I am not saying that journalists need to pretend to be nice for the sake of it, or that they shouldn't respond strongly (even sarcastically!) to criticism they think is wrong-headed. I *am* saying that they need to think a little more deeply about the sort of image they convey via social media and not just work from the assumption, as happened in the above exchange, that all criticism is a personal attack, or even an attack at all. We can see the projection: Priest accuses Jericho of being overly sensitive when in fact, given the reasonableness of Jericho's comment about tiered subscriptions, it is Priest who is being thin-skinned and precious.

The only way to bridge these divides between audience members and journalists is with more and better contact between the two groups, and not just on social media. And there is some evidence that journalists accept this. Senior figures such as George Megalogenis, Katharine Murphy, and Lenore Taylor have all spoken about the centrality of the audience in what they do and have made efforts to make their work more transparent. The Walkley survey I cited earlier also addressed audience engagement. A lot of ambivalence was expressed, and the authors noted that '[g]reater interactivity with readers raises unexpected practical and professional challenges for newsrooms. It adds to staff and resource needs and requires a new approach to editorial leadership'. Yet, 'overall, the journalists we spoke to see concrete benefits in opening up the news process to outsiders'.

I have mentioned that I have similar concerns about time and costs, but I don't see how journalists can hope to maintain any credibility in their claim to be a fourth estate unless they and, as importantly, their employers are willing to confront these problems.

I personally like the idea put forward by Dan Hind in his book *The Return of the Public: democracy, power and the case for media reform*. He wants the public right there in the newsroom, helping to commission the stories. He argues, 'Once we engage directly in the production of information in a shared institutional context we begin to develop the knowledge and the self-knowledge necessary to guide further political change.' Further, he notes, 'This process of public commissioning will have the effect of making more, and different, facts generally available' and that '[i]nstead of the situation we have now, where the population is reconciled to the demands of the "public interest" through the combined efforts of journalists, politicians and public relations experts, under the system I propose the general population secures the means to transform itself into a public'.

If this sounds hopelessly idealistic, consider that such things are already happening. *The Guardian* in Britain has opened up aspects of its story budgets to the public, while inviting comments from readers on what stories to cover and how to cover them via its *Newsdesk live* blog. 'Each day on the Newsdesk live blog, *The Guardian*'s national news team will bring you the news as we break it, explain how we choose what we report and why — and ask you to get involved. Send us your ideas, evidence and experiences to help shape our coverage,' they tell us on the website.

*The Atlantic* is another to go down this path with their Open Wire initiative, which they explain this way:

> We've been conducting a little experiment of editing the site on the site. As with many web news operations, *The Atlantic* Wire is mostly edited via terse messages in a group chat room. Editors and writers spend the day logged onto Campfire pitching story ideas, exchanging links and keeping everyone up to date on the news of the day. So we had a thought: why not move that out into the open and let anyone who wants to take part?
>
> If you'd like to suggest a story or merely kibbitz all you need to do is login in with a Disqus account. We'll see how this turns out.

Some organisations have been even more adventurous, though the results show that while engagement with the audience might be a desirable goal, it is no panacea. The CEO of the Journal Register Company, John Paton, is a salutary example. Like a lot of its US counterparts, the Register was a moribund newspaper company suffering under the onslaught of online media, with falling income and demoralised staff. Paton instigated a number of innovations, including one he called the Ben Franklin Project. In essence, the project allowed readers to commission journalists to write stories, in very much the way that Dan Hind was suggesting. Let me quote Paton himself:

> Yes, the reporters will still report and the editors will still edit. The difference in the Ben Franklin project is that the journalists will be accountable throughout — not simply after the story reaches deadline and is delivered to the audience. The staff members involved in the Ben Franklin project will ensure their reporting process is transparent so as to encourage full participation from the audience. Reporters will document their newsgathering online thus providing the audience opportunity to question, guide and join the process. All of this will start with the assigning process.
>
> To truly engage our readership we must know they are interested in reading, watching and consuming what is reported. The legacy measurements of circulation, sales and even the modern metrics of unique visitors and page views

only measure reader interest after the fact. By providing a platform where users can suggest stories, vote for story assignments and/or contribute (information, sources, data, etc.), the Ben Franklin Project will create an open-sourced assignment desk. And, the process will continue as readers track story developments online. Stories that [are] not judged worthy by the audience could be dismissed while those that may have been dismissed under a legacy model could find new life.

I'm struck by his comment about the shortfall in the efficacy of measurements of circulation. As I noted in the previous chapter, it is not enough to rely upon these after-the-fact quantifications without also engaging with the audience beforehand to see if there are simply *other* things they might be interested in.

The Register also tried some other experiments. Journalist Margaret Simons, in her book *Journalism at the Crossroads: crisis and opportunity for the press*, points out that 'the most daring innovation', the one that 'most alarms the editors and journalists I have mentioned it to', occurred when the Register opened its newsrooms to the public in November 2011. 'It started with *The Register Citizen* in Torrington, Connecticut, a former mill town of about 40,000 people,' Simons writes. 'A cafe was established — not on the street side of the security barriers like those on the ground floors of *The Age* and the *Herald Sun*, but right in the heart of the newsroom.' Paton also appointed a full-time editor to 'support existing community bloggers and citizen journalists, and to recruit new ones', thus underlining the organisation's commitment not just to their most engaged readers but also to the community they served and the local news they valued.

But the final results were mixed. The Journal Register Company went from financial basket case to modest financial success. Simons records:

> In May 2011, John Paton announced to his employees that, while the goal had been to hit US$40 million in profit in 2010, that target was exceeded — profit was US$41 million. Under the profit-sharing arrangement that he had promised during his first days with the company, all employees would get an extra week's pay. 'Not bad for a bankrupt, beat up old newspaper company people had written off as dead in 2009,' he wrote.

With things looking healthier, the group was sold to the hedge fund Alden Global Capital.

That was the good news. The bad news was that in 2012, under the new ownership, the company filed for bankruptcy. Supporters of Paton's 'digital first' strategy maintain that this was a strategic move designed to 'reboot' the company, a way of redirecting resources, and certainly the Register wouldn't be the first company to use a bankruptcy filing in this way. Paton himself told *The New York Times*: 'From a business perspective, it's the absolute right thing to do.' Others were less sanguine. Writing in *The Guardian*, columnist and media writer Michael Wolff said, 'The problem ... was that, so far, the digital strategy had, from a revenue standpoint, not become all that significant to the company — you'd be hard-pressed to find much value there.'

The final chapter of Paton's experiments at the Register has not been written, but it is clear enough that audience engagement is no guaranteed cure for the malaise affecting newspapers. However, given that the basic commercial formula has become dependent on getting the audience to pay for their journalism, it is hard to see an 'audience first' approach as anything other than an essential part of a forward-looking business strategy.

Margaret Simons makes the point that the Journal Register Company 'correctly identified that the key asset arising from its history was not its business position but its relationship to its readers. And it is using a technology that is all about relationships to build that asset through every kind of journalistic method'. Similarly, as former editor and journalist John L. Robinson has said about his experiences at the *News & Record* newspaper in North Carolina: 'There may be other reasons [I got things wrong]. Complacency, however, wasn't one of them. I never felt as if we were in decent shape, that we could rest, that we had reached our destination. Instead, I was like a kid running around with my arms outstretched thinking I was an airplane.' He was certain about one missed opportunity, however: 'Had

I organized monthly meetings with the public to hear how we could serve them better, it would have improved our journalism, and I would have been a better steward of their newspaper.'

James Janega of the *Chicago Tribune* also stresses the importance of audience engagement. In an article on the Poynter website, he argues that 'social media is only part of the equation. Digital can be a proxy for interaction, but it works better when paired with the real thing'. He cites five initiatives his paper has instigated in order to enhance its relationship with its audience: take corrections and clarifications seriously, explain the news-gathering process, hold community-based events, engage in a conversation with your audience, and embrace social media.

Janega acknowledges that not everything they do works, but the point is, 'It was always about experimenting, not failure or success.' From my perspective, the simple fact that a news organisation is willing to even *try* things like this conveys that they are serious about what they are doing and respect their audience. Again, it is not about some phony sense of civility or pandering to what demographic research shows that people 'want'. It is about according your audience the respect of talking to them, not down to them.

But none of these innovations have a chance of success, or indeed get us heading back towards David Simon's world of high-end journalism, if news outlets continue to lose staff in the way described earlier by Laura Tingle.

While it may seem obvious that an organisation needs to downsize when revenue is tight, there comes a point beyond which such an approach leads to a self-fulfilling downward spiral.

So it is interesting to see uber-investor Warren Buffett, whose company has recently been making strategic investments in local US newspaper groups, arguing for expansion rather than contraction. In a comment after my own heart, he says that the newspaper business isn't a widget business. It isn't like other industries he invests in, but nevertheless he is not motivated by charity or personal obsession. 'It's not a soft-headed business decision,' he told US media reporter Howard Kurtz. 'It's not going to move the needle at Berkshire Hathaway [his investment company]. If it were the widget business, I wouldn't do it. The kind of earnings we'll draw from our newspaper properties will be a very tiny fraction of, say, Burlington Railroad. But it's not a dumb decision financially.'

In his 2012 annual letter to his investors, Buffett said of newspapers:

Wherever there is a pervasive sense of community, a paper that serves the special informational needs of that community will remain indispensable to a significant portion of its residents. Even a valuable product, however, can self-destruct from a faulty business strategy. And that process has been underway during the past decade at almost all papers of size. Publishers — including Berkshire in Buffalo — have offered their paper free on the Internet while charging meaningful sums for the physical specimen. How could this lead to anything other than a sharp and steady drop in sales of the printed product?

I wonder if executives at *The Age* and *The Sydney Morning Herald* have read that.

Just as interestingly, Buffett also notes: 'We do not believe that success will come from cutting either the news content or frequency of publication. Indeed, skimpy news coverage will almost certainly lead to skimpy readership.' He observes that 'the less-than-daily publication that is now being tried in some large towns or cities — while it may improve profits in the short term — seems certain to diminish the papers' relevance over time', adding, 'Our goal is to keep our papers loaded with content of interest to our readers and to be paid appropriately by those who find us useful, whether the product they view is in their hands or on the Internet.'

Amen to that, because what is happening is that journalism is being de-skilled. More and more content is being generated not by journalists but by their doppelgangers in the public relations industry, while journalists themselves are being subjected to grinding work regimes that make it all but impossible for them to pursue long-term investigations, or even perform basic fact-checking.

As one tiny example, consider this email, made public by the ABC's *Media Watch*, which was sent from Fairfax management to staff, explaining what will be expected of them as *The Age* and *The Sydney Morning Herald* change from a broadsheet format to the smaller 'compact', or tabloid, form:

> I know by now you are all used to newsroom challenges and have worked wonders to meet them. Well, it's only three weeks till we all face another big one when the Herald goes compact …
>
> Weekday papers will have between 17–19 early general news pages. Each one of those pages will need between one and three stories, and most will require illustration with photos or graphics …
>
> So, in a nutshell, whereas, there were some 18 stories and 10 briefs in today's … broadsheet pages, we're going to need to generate at the very least double that number, and preferably three times for choice and balance, to fill the equivalent compact.
>
> Given the number of pages, there will also be strict page deadlines, with the early pages going 'off stone' by 2.30pm, which will place new demands on copy flow.

I don't know what's more extraordinary: the extra workload being dumped on the journalists, or the casual way in which the demand is delivered.

The aim of this book is not to pretend that I know better than anyone else how to run a profitable media company.

In fact, the whole point is that I *don't* know: no one does, and nor is there a single answer. This is precisely why the industry needs as much input as it can get.

In thinking about this, I was struck by the following comments by Abe Epton, who went from working for Google News — that ultimate online aggregator and compiler of information — to the *Chicago Tribune*, an old-fashioned newspaper trying to survive in the world that Google helped create. Epton highlights some of the things that I think make the increasingly threatened newsroom worth saving, and in so doing, he echoes my argument about the impossibility (or extreme difficulty) of smaller, online-only titles and their citizen journalists replacing the institutions of the mainstream media:

> While things were still fresh, I wanted to think about the things that strike me about my new, old-media gig and why I think people interested in code and civic society should really think about joining a newspaper — yes, a newspaper (or any media outlet) — in 2013.
>
> To begin with, the newsroom is one of the most connected places I've ever seen. Information flows through it constantly, via phones and police scanners and loud clackety-noise-making machines of indeterminate purpose (not the nearby typewriter), as well as the ubiquitous Tweetdeck and Chartbeat screens. We have our morning meetings on a television stage elevated in the middle of the room.
>
> But it's the informal networks, the overheard chats

among reporters and editors and the one-way conversations with sources, that provide a unique and fascinating education on how stories are put together and what's going on in the city.

Epton's comments are a great reminder of babies and bathwater, of the basic paradox lurking in the soft folds of the culture of many democratic institutions — that what can appear, to the casual (and especially, the technocratic) observer, to be faults and inefficiencies are in fact practices and habits that have developed to keep the whole thing working. They are a reminder that we shouldn't be looking for ways to fix these things, only improve them, and that we throw out these layered, established, and deep sources of information and debate at our democratic peril.

For as long as I have been thinking about this stuff, I have been convinced that we need better ways for ordinary voters to be heard in public discussions. That's what my PhD thesis was about, it was what a large part of my blogging at *Surfdom* and *Blogocracy* was about, and it is what this book is about. In a democracy, you either take the right of people to participate in the running of their country seriously or you don't. There are endless excuses the political class use in order to rationalise their lack of commitment to that simple proposition, but we shouldn't be fooled. In the end, all the excuses fall flat.

So it is no use saying, as the media often does, that people are disengaged. It is more important that journalists and editors examine the ways in which they themselves engage and consider their own culpability when the audience turns away.

It is no use invoking the technocratic response, which says either leave it to the experts or become expert yourself before participating in public discussion. That approach excludes people from the very means of acquiring the knowledge that the technocrats lament is missing: public discussion. It utterly confuses ends and means, too. Yes, we need experts to advise on the best ways to achieve particular outcomes, but the outcomes themselves are for the people to decide, expert or not.

It is no use taking the academic approach and bemoaning the lack of civics training in schools. All the civics training in the world is not going help if people still lack the opportunity to be heard in the public square.

It is no use taking the approach of the political parties and commissioning yet another poll or focus group in order to 'understand' what people are thinking; political leaders need to get out in communities and re-engage with the public by making their parties more attractive so that people want to join them.

It is certainly no use taking the approach of the new-media enthusiast and proclaiming (as I have in the past) that 'if you build it they will come'. The figures show they won't, or at least not in a broad enough cross-section to make a difference. By all means, start your blog and activate your Twitter account, hit the streets with your phone camera, and put the footage on YouTube, but realise that unless your work can engage and motivate a *general* audience, it is extremely limited in what it can achieve.

There are some brilliant success stories out there in the field of new media in Australia, but they tend to be examples of 'verticals', which is what the industry calls the various niche reporting areas — everything from business through to sports. We can point to the groundbreaking success of *mUmBRELLA*, which deals with the media and advertising industry, and is a go-to site for many who work in the field. There is Alan Kohler's Business Spectator group, recently sold to News Limited, which, as the name suggests, is dedicated to reporting and commentary on business matters. There is Renai LeMay's *Delimiter* site, which covers tech issues, including the way governments and oppositions deal with policy in this area. *Delimiter* is notable, I think, for its innovative approach to separating straight journalism from commentary, by placing the commentary directly after the news piece. It's a model I would like to see the mainstream adopt, because it adds to transparency. As in: here are the basic facts of the story, but now read this and see how I, the journalist, understand those facts.

Perhaps most interestingly and most significantly of all, we have the growing segment of so-called mummy blogs, particularly *Mamamia*, run by Mia Freedman. The term mummy blogger has been used as a putdown, to disparage the sites for dealing with 'women's issues', but I think it is fair to say that the sites themselves have somewhat embraced the term in an attempt to draw the poison. Regardless, they are beginning to play an important role in the media landscape, aided and abetted by the fact that politicians are starting to take them seriously. Julia Gillard, for example, in a series of specially arranged interviews, used *Mamamia* as a way of speaking to the site's particular demographic.

These smaller sites do a fantastic job within their respective fields, often a better job than their mainstream counterparts. But alone or in combination, I don't think they can be seen as a replacement for that cornerstone function of democratic oversight that is at the heart of the mainstream's claims to be a fourth estate. What's more, the people who run these sites have had careers as media professionals; some, such as Alan Kohler and Mia Freedman, at senior levels. Not one of them is an amateur who just happened to start a blog that took off. Neither are any of them what enthusiasts mean when they talk about 'citizen journalists'. All of which suggests that raw talent and specialised knowledge can only get you so far.

Again, democracies need a mainstream media more than they need citizen journalists. But surely the ultimate lesson of the last decade is that the mainstream media needs to change. I don't just mean that media companies need to embrace the new technologies and learn to work across a range of platforms: most are already doing that. I mean they need to reinvent their fundamental understanding of what it is they are doing and how they do it, while keeping in place the skills and attitudes that allow them to function as a fourth estate. They have to question every assumption they have about what constitutes news, how it is gathered, and how it is presented. And I believe that the best way for them to do that is by better engaging with the people they are asking to pay for their product. Journalists and editors have to accord audiences the respect they deserve and be willing to listen to them and learn from them *before* they write their stories, not just count the clicks afterwards. It's as radical and as mundane as that.

# Acknowledgements

*Where the clouds are like headlines*
*On a new front page sky*
Tom Waits

The first people I want to thank are all those readers who, by whatever means, stumbled across my early forays into the blogosphere and who have stuck around for over a decade now, reading and commenting on the things I have written. I include in that all those early Australian (mostly political) bloggers, such as Rob Corr, Amanda Rose, John Quiggin, Ken Parish, Jason Soon, Chris Sheil, Gianna Huesch, Gareth Parker, Mark Bahnisch, Helen Smart, Zoe Bowman, and others too numerous to mention. They were pioneers — groundbreakers — and they rarely get the credit they deserve. I hope they enjoy the story told in these pages.

I want to thank Hugh Martin for his early faith in me, for his ongoing encouragement, and for reading parts of this book and making them better. Mark Davis, Jim Parker, and Greg Jericho also read early drafts of various chapters and offered sage and pertinent advice that undoubtedly saved me from error and embarrassment. On that subject, I also want to thank Julia Carlomagno from Scribe and Sonja Heijn for their incredible work as editors. They were gracious and professional, and it was a pleasure to work with them. Any remaining problems readers find with the text are there because I failed to properly heed the advice of all these people.

Many of the ideas discussed here had their origins in articles published in a number of outlets over the last ten years, pieces I draw on and sometimes quote here. My thanks go to Jonathan Green and Chip Rolley, past and present editors of *The Drum*, who have given me the space to think out loud about issues to do with the media. Jane Gilmore at *The King's Tribune* has also been incredibly supportive. Josh Fanning of *Collect* magazine is another who has published work upon which I draw here. The phrase 'the new front page' is one I read in an article by Katharine Murphy and I liked it so much I borrowed it for the title of this book. I also want to thank Foong Ling Kong, who been generous with her time and wise with her counsel. I owe a special gratitude to Henry Rosenbloom for letting me pitch this book to him and for agreeing to publish it.

My family has been incredible. I thank in particular my amazing son, Noah, who is not only a joy to be around but is also an inspiration in his dedication to his chosen field of dance. And I thank my wife, Tanya, for her love and support stretching back over more than half a lifetime. What did I do to deserve such a gift?

## The Rise of the Fifth Estate
### GREG JERICHO

---

**The first book to examine the emergence of social media
as a new force in the coverage of Australian politics**

Using original research, Greg Jericho reveals who makes up the Australian
political blogosphere, and tackles head-on some of its key developments —
the way that Australia's journalists and federal politicians use social media
and digital news, the motivations of bloggers and tweeters, the treatment
of female participants, and the eruption of Twitter wars.

'An illuminating and, for the most part, entertaining snapshot of where
the new media landscape and politics meet.' *The Canberra Times*

'An important contribution to our knowledge of how Australian
politics and the Australian media operate, and a book that
all media professionals, and indeed anyone who is interested in politics
and the media, should have on their shelves.' *Bookseller and Publisher*

SCRIBE    Seriously good books.
scribepublications.com.au

## *Stop Press*
### RACHEL BUCHANAN

---

**The second book in Scribe's Media Chronicles series**

A unique insider's account of the rise and slow decline of print,
this insightful, passionate book investigates one of the most
fundamental transitions in the Australian media today. It exposes
the brutal cost-cutting measures of companies intent on squeezing
every drop of profit from print before they turn to digital, and examines
the consequences for those affected: for it is not only the journalists
and editors who are losing their jobs, but also printers, paper-makers,
and distributors whose livelihood is disappearing.

'The unfolding collapse of the great city-newspaper business model is a
commercial and civic tragedy. But, as Buchanan reveals, it's also a human
tragedy that is upending the professional lives of too many fine journalists.'
ERIC BEECHER

SCRIBE Seriously good books.
scribepublications.com.au